SHADOWS

Based on a true story

A.J. TAIRE

Pageleaf Publishing Ltd
www.pageleafpublishing.com

Copyright © 2025 by A. J. Taire

First published in the United Kingdom by
Pageleaf Publishing Ltd., London

This is a work of fiction. Names, characters, places, and incidents are either the product of the author's imagination or are used fictitiously. Any resemblance to actual persons, living or dead, events, or locales is purely coincidental.

All rights reserved. No part of this book may be reproduced, distributed, or transmitted in any form or by any means, including photocopying, recording, or other electronic or mechanical methods, without the prior written permission of the publisher, except in the case of brief quotations embodied in critical reviews and certain other noncommercial uses permitted by copyright law.

ISBN (Paperback): 978-1-917833-03-5
First Pageleaf Publishing Print Edition: October 2025

Printed in the United Kingdom

For Njide Maureen Onyiuke

PROLOGUE

I used to be full of joy and without a care in the world, but that would be expected at thirteen, right? Teenagers rarely have much to worry about at that age. We all grow up under different circumstances, but certain things in life inevitably shape who we become. At that time, I was preparing for my Junior Secondary School exams in Nigeria, excited to go to the next stage in secondary school. JSS exams are crucial in the secondary school journey in Nigeria. As at this point we decide what route we would like to pursue. We could go down the science or art route, depending on our skills.

For those in England, Junior secondary school exams would be the equivalent of being in year nine. At thirteen, I was one of the smallest in my class, I was so tiny that one would miss me if they walked into my class.

You might assume that being small made me quiet and reserved, but I wasn't one to hide, I was outspoken and gregarious, and my classmates believed this was my defence mechanism to avoid bullying, however I wasn't the type to stir up trouble.

I had two best friends Isioma, whom we called Isi and Halima fondly called Matar Kulikuli, we called her that because she loved to eat kulikuli, a popular Nigerian snack made with groundnuts and spices.

I was born in Lagos, and my family has lived in Lagos for as long as I can remember. Growing up, I loved helping my mother make Zobo a fruit drink made from hibiscus flowers and fruits. Occasionally, I would help her deliver it to family friends within our estate. Our estate wasn't particularly large, but it was easy to get lost in it. There was always something happening, people coming in and going out of the estate, some of them residents, other visitors, and of course, hawkers who came to sell their wares from fruits to household accessories. It wasn't a very safe place to grow up in as back then security wasn't as tight as it is in the modern estates we see today.

Now, let me introduce you to my family.

Ours wasn't really a large one. My father was the head of the household, and my mother was deeply devoted to her role as a wife. I have four strong sisters: Lola, the twins; Taiye and Kehinde and then there's Alaba. I, Eyimofe Olamide Idowu, is the only one among the children with three names, thanks to my maternal grandmother. We were very close, and even now after all these years, I still miss her dearly.

Everyone calls me Mide, which is a shortened version of my middle name, Olamide.

My paternal grandma lives with us, as her only surviving child, my father was very precious to her, having lost her other children at a young age. Granny as she is fondly called is an amazing and very strong woman.

It's difficult not to like her.

Speaking of Granny, if you're curious to know how she and my mom get along, it's the classic mother-in-law and daughter-in-law relationship. You know, the kind where the mother-in-law is seen as a "witch" and the daughter-in-law is never quite good enough. It was exactly like that! But honestly, their bickering could be quite entertaining at times.

I think I got away with a lot because my grandmother had a soft spot for me and loved going against my mom. Even though my family is from the Itsekiri tribe in Delta State, we were born and bred in Lagos. Before I forget, my mother is from Lagos state. Being all girls in the family meant we had to be tough, especially as family members often tried to take advantage of us, particularly on my father's side. I was the worst of all my siblings with a sharp tongue that often got me into trouble, which never stopped me from standing up for myself.

Looking back now, my life has been full of unexpected twists—perhaps dramatic enough to be the plot of a movie someday. These past thirty years have taught me countless lessons that have shaped who I am today.

My name is Eyimofe Olamide Idowu Omatseye, and this is my story.

CHAPTER ONE

August 1997

It started out like any ordinary day, a Thursday.

I was excited as this was the last day before the school broke up for the summer holidays.

I was eager to go home not because I was excited for the break but because, I had narrowly missed being punished by a Senior for something I did not do.

I wasn't even the one who caused the trouble; but typical, I had to speak which put me on Senior Anuli's Radar.

Why do I always have to speak?

Would it be hard to just mind my business and not get involved in other people's issues?

I had tried to explain to Senior Anuli and her friends, but they wouldn't hear of it and were determined to teach me a lesson.

God forbid they catch me, wicked seniors, who delighted in lording it over us juniors.

As soon as I burst into our compound, I slammed the gate shut, sliding the latch into place before peeking through the cracks to see if that wicked Senior Anuli had followed.

"Mide!" my mother's shout had me turning round, a guilty look on my face. "I knew it was you! What trouble have you caused now?" she yelled, waving her hands in the air.

There were times I genuinely felt like my mother didn't like me at all. She was always finding fault in everything I did, always blaming me even if I was innocent.

"Nothing, Mum," I muttered, glancing over my shoulder, hoping Senior Anuli would not stop here on her way home.

"So why are you running and who are you running from?" She asked, folding her arms as she studied me.

"I am not running Mum," I replied, hoping she would stop asking me questions as I tried to edge past her.

"Is that so? You'd better not be lying to me. If I find out you've done something, you won't believe what I'll do to you today," she warned, wagging her finger at me before heading back inside.

As I stood there, simmering with resentment, I watched her walk away, her footsteps echoing across the lawn. Just as she reached the house, my grandmother emerged, her eyes flashing with a fierce determination.

"What's going on here?" Granny demanded, her voice firm but controlled. "The girl said she didn't do anything. Didn't you hear her?" She glared at my mother, annoyed. "Why must you always pick on her?" My Granny's words hung in the air, a stern rebuke that only added to my mother's anger.

"Mama, please let me handle my own child," my mother responded dismissively, without pausing to acknowledge my Granny as she turned and walked back into the house.

"Mtscheew! Your own child." Grandma hissed, walking toward me.

It was hard, hard not to feel hurt at my mother's attitude toward me. No matter what I did, my mother would never see the good in me. Okay, maybe I was a little opinionated, but I wasn't a bad kid.

I did well in school, better than my sisters, always coming top in my class, yet, instead of praise, I always got scolded for acting out simply because I was brilliant. If I came back from school with a nine and half over ten score, she would ask what happened to the remaining half. There was never any praise or encouragement from her.

Children make mistakes, right? Isn't that part of growing up?

The sound of the kitchen door slamming jolted me from my thoughts, and I turned around to see my mother heading back toward me, holding my dad's whip, popularly called "koboko".

You see that whip, every Nigerian kid from the eighties and nineties knew what that meant. The "koboko" was more than just a whip, it was the ultimate symbol of discipline. The very sight of it could make any child including my stubborn self-behave instantly.

We called it "the reset button."

Granny saw it too and quickly stepped in.

"Toke, what is this? Do you really want to flog this child? What has she done?" she shouted, stepping in front of my mother.

Mama, please let me be," my mother said, though her tone suggested she wasn't as calm as she was trying to appear.

"Let you be? How can I let you be?" Granny said defiantly, throwing herself between us and pushing her chest forward like a protective shield. "Come on, hit me first! Go on!"

The whole scene was so surreal that it made me momentarily forget the danger I was in. But then I remembered the koboko and frantically tried to open the gate. Panic gripped me as the gate refused to budge.

Just then, the kitchen door opened, and my sister Kenny came running out just as my mother closed in on me, her hands raised above her head, koboko in hand as Kenny quickly stepped in, positioning herself between us.

"Mummy, what is it? She hasn't even entered the house! She just got back from school!" Kenny said, pushing me towards my Granny, who pulled me away from my angry mum.

"Don't you dare try to defend her!" my mum snapped.

"Why not?" Granny chimed in, still holding her ground.

"What has she done?" my sister asked my mum, who was still glaring at me.

"I don't know, ask her." my mother replied, glaring at me.

Kenny turned to me. "Mide, what happened? What did you do?"

"Nothing. I just came home from school and mum assumed I did something wrong because I ran into the compound," I explained, still hiding behind my sister.

"Is that so?" my mum asked, still looking at me with suspicion.

"I didn't do anything, mum." I insisted.

"Mum, she didn't do anything. Just let her be." Kenny said, trying to diffuse the situation.

"Exactly! She just got home, and you come rushing out with a whip to beat her!" Granny shouted, eyeballing my mum.

"Alright, fine. But if I find out she's lying, Kenny, I'll deal with you too!" mum warned, clearly still sceptical.

"Mide go inside," Kenny said to me.

I didn't need to be told twice.

I was grateful Kenny had arrived when she did; if it had been any of my other siblings, I'd likely be nursing my bruised backside by now, or worse, facing mum's wrath for who-knows-how-long.

Kenny always had a way of calming mum down, when the rest of us couldn't. There was something about Kenny's calm demeanour that seemed to soothe mum's nerves and make her see reason, thank goodness for that.

Hmm, imagine after escaping from Senior Anuli, I come home to my mother's beating! See, I would have run back to school to accept the punishment from the seniors, any punishment but my mum whipping me is acceptable.

"Come on, let's go inside," Granny said, giving me a reassuring smile that made me feel like everything was going to be okay. "Bless you, my child," she said to Kenny, throwing a sharp glance at my mother that seemed to say, "*Wicked Woman*", as she walked by her.

Smiling, I walked into the house with my head held high, feeling like a princess with Granny right behind me as my loyal supporter. I had escaped a major tsunami! Any fear I had melted away the moment Kenny had spoken up for me, and I couldn't wait for Alaba to return so we could relive the drama and excitement of the afternoon. I was already imagining the animated retelling of the story, complete with hand gestures and exaggerated expressions, and I couldn't help but smile at the thought.

Thank God for Granny and Kenny.

* * *

One would have thought after the drama that afternoon, I would mind my business but not me, trouble drew me like a magnet, anywhere trouble went, I followed.

I had just finished folding my clothes when I heard singing from the kitchen.

Immediately, the little gossip in me took over and I ran as fast as I could to the kitchen.

"What's going on?" I asked, as I burst into the kitchen to find my mum chopping vegetables on the table.

Ah, big mistake, that Kenny was not anywhere near the kitchen, I realised.

Instantly I began backing out of the kitchen.

"What's it to you, little gossip?" Mum replied, eyeing me suspiciously, though I could see the corners of her mouth twitching in amusement.

Granny sighed dramatically. "Ah, ah! Don't you see she just wants to know?"

"Are you laughing at me?" Mum asked, nodding towards me.

I knew better than to stick around, whenever she asked that, it usually meant trouble wasn't far behind and since she hadn't gotten her way in the afternoon, she would look for any opportunity to beat me.

"No, mum. I wasn't laughing at you," I quickly replied, backing away.

"Oh mum, leave her alone now," Kenny said, from behind me laughing as she walked into the kitchen.

She smiled at me, and for a moment, I couldn't help but think how lucky I was to have her as my sister.

"I've got news, but I want you to guess what it is," she said, her eyes twinkling with excitement.

"You got a new job?" I asked, already knowing that wasn't it.

"Better! One more guess," she teased.

"You're having a baby?" I said, practically shouting in excitement.

"Shut up!" my mum snapped at me, her voice sharp. "This your mouth won't kill you! What baby? Is she married yet?"

"Mummy, relax. I was the one who told her to guess," Kenny said, defending me as always.

"Anyway, no more babies just yet," Kenny said with a wink, holding up her hand. It took me a second to notice the ring on her finger, and when I did, I screamed in delight, hugging her tightly.

"Is it Uncle Segun?" I asked excitedly.

"No, it's brother Aliu. Of course it's Segun. Who else would it be?" my sister replied, laughing at my enthusiasm.

"Congratulations! I'm moving in with you when you get married!" I declared, matter of fact, ignoring the warning glance my mum was giving me from where she stood.

I ignored her, smiling at my sister who smiled warmly at me. I loved Kenny, she was my hero, and I couldn't help but feel that everything would be alright if she was around.

Chapter Two

"Kenny is getting married!" That was the first thing I blurted out the moment Alaba stepped into the living room.

"Amebo!" Mum scolded from behind me, but I was too thrilled to care what she thought, instead, I ran to Alaba, grabbed her hand, and pulled her over to Kenny, who was laughing at my excitement.

"Is it true?" Alaba asked, her voice filled with a mixture of awe and disbelief.

"Yes, it's true. I'm getting married," Kenny confirmed with a soft smile.

Alaba squealed and threw her arms around her, hugging her tightly, eager not to be left out. I followed without hesitation, embracing both fiercely, forgetting, no, ignoring the fact that Mum was still in the room. I lived for moment like this, full of laughter, closeness, and unfiltered joy. But they never lasted long as Mum always found a way to puncture the happiness with a snide remark or a withering look.

Strangely, today she didn't, she just stood there, speechless for once.

Still, I knew if *I* had been the one squealing like Alaba, she would have thrown a newspaper at me and muttered something about me being "too loud" or "unladylike."

But today, all she did was watch.

"Where's Granny?" Alaba asked.

"She's gone to her room," Kenny replied.

"Thank goodness," Mum muttered under her breath.

Kenny and I exchanged knowing glances before Alaba excitedly tugged her toward Granny's room.

* * *

Mum had just finished setting the table for dinner when Dad walked in, his usual big smile lighting up his face as soon as he saw me.

I ran to him instantly, took his briefcase from him, and threw myself into his arms.

"Easy!" he laughed, staggering a bit before hugging me tightly. "How was school today?"

"Fantastic!" I beamed.

"My English lady," he teased, ruffling my hair. "Can't you just say 'fine' like the rest of us common folks?"

"No, Daddy, I can't. If I don't speak like this, how will I pass my exams?" I replied with a grin.

He laughed, placing me gently back on the floor as my Mum materialised by his side, giving him a soft hug. Smiling sheepishly, I backed away, giving them a little space, before heading out of the living room to call my siblings for dinner.

* * *

That night, for the first time in ages, the entire family sat together at the dining table, even Granny, who usually insisted on eating in her room, was there, sitting quietly at the head of the table. As was the case, the no-talking rule at dinner hung over us like a heavy curtain, one Mum enforced with an iron will. It was especially hard on Alaba and I who always had something to say. If we weren't allowed to talk, we fidgeted; I'd bounce my legs under the table, and Alaba would wiggle in her seat like she had ants in her pants.

But tonight, I wasn't going to let anyone steal my moment.

"We have news for you, Daddy!" I squealed, ignoring Mum's warning look from across the table.

"You know the rules," Dad began gently, but I couldn't hold it in.

"Kenny is getting married!" I blurted out, practically bouncing in my seat.

The look on my mother's face was priceless, a mix of shock and disbelief. My siblings burst into laughter, even Dad chuckled before the weight of the announcement hit him.

"Wait, what?" he asked, turning to Kenny.

"She's getting married!" I repeated, unable to contain my joy.

"Aah, these children!" Mum groaned, exasperated. "Is nothing private in this house anymore?"

"Mum, how can this be a secret?" I replied cheekily. "And even if it were, how could we keep something like this from Daddy?"

My Mum stared at me for a long moment before shaking her head. "Just be quiet. Did I ask you to speak? Learn to talk only when you're spoken to."

"Toke, leave her alone," Dad said, still smiling. "Wasn't it the same with your siblings? Didn't they announce it to the whole neighbourhood when I came to ask for your hand?"

"Timi, that was different," Mum huffed, brushing it off.

"No, it wasn't," he said. "Be glad you can see your siblings in your children."

Then he turned to Kenny, whose cheeks were glowing. "Well, Kenny, this is truly good news. I'm glad Segun finally proposed. Congratulations, my dear. We'll talk more in my room after dinner."

"Yes, Daddy. Thank you," Kenny replied, as she smiled at my dad.

After that, Dad lifted the dinner ban.

The table exploded with chatter, laughter, and excitement over Kenny's engagement much to Mum's annoyance.

But for once, none of us cared.

* * *

The rest of the weekend was filled with nonstop discussions about Kenny's wedding. Every conversation somehow circled back to the big day, and it seemed like there was always someone in the house debating a detail or offering a suggestion. Alaba and I would sit on the edge of our seats, excitedly listening to all the plans. The excitement was contagious, but there was no denying that the conversations were exhausting too, especially for someone like Mum, who was already treating the wedding like it was the event of the century.

"Kenny, we need to start thinking about asoebi," Mum said one evening as we all sat in the living room, she had a notepad in front of her, already scribbling ideas down.

Kenny looked up, her face amused but a little tired. "Mum, we haven't even picked a date yet and Segun isn't back till next week to come and ask for my hand formally before his parents come."

"And that's the problem! Why hasn't he come yet?" Mum snapped, clicking her pen as she looked around at all of us. "Time waits for no one. We need to organize everything, including picking fabrics and planning the gifts. You know people will be expecting something nice."

Alaba and I exchanged a glance.

The excitement in the air made it hard for us to sit still.

Kenny's wedding plans were far more interesting than anything we had going on in our lives now, but Kenny was right, we were going too fast, Segun hadn't even come to the house, the poor man had only just proposed and yet here we were planning his wedding but none of us dared say that to our mother.

"Ah, Mummy, you're already planning gifts? Shouldn't we first talk to the in-laws?" Kenny asked, laughing softly.

Mum waved her hand dismissively. "Don't worry about that. Your father and I will handle the in-laws. We'll meet them when the time is right. For now, I need to make sure I'm dressed better than Segun's mother. It's my duty as the mother of the bride."

I couldn't help but laugh. "Mummy, are you competing with the in-laws already?"

"It's not competition, Mide," Mum said, giving me a pointed look. "I'm simply making sure they know that my daughter's family is well prepared. If we don't put in the effort, people will talk."

Dad, who had been quietly reading his newspaper, chuckled from behind it. "Toke don't start this competition now. Let's meet them first."

Mum ignored him. "Timi, I was thinking we should book the church hall for the traditional wedding. The compound will be too small for the gathering we have planned. You know Kenny is the first daughter to get married in Lagos, and the whole family will be there."

"The whole family and the rest of Lagos," I muttered under my breath, earning a glare from Mum.

"Don't worry, Toke, we'll look into it," Dad said, putting his paper down and nodding. "But let's not get ahead of ourselves. We'll see what the in-laws want as well."

Mum huffed, but we all knew she was right. Kenny was her favourite child, and we all knew that she would spend every penny she had on that wedding. Alaba nudged me under the table and whispered, "Mum's going to act like she's the one getting married."

I snickered, but it was true.

Mum was acting like she was the one getting married, God help us.

Chapter Three

Before we knew it, the day of Kenny's traditional wedding arrived, bright and sunny, as if the sky had put on its best attire. It was one of those perfect days when the air seemed almost eager, buzzing with anticipation for the festivities ahead.

By the time I woke up, the excitement at home was already hanging thickly in the air. Our father, in his wisdom, had insisted the wedding take place in our compound. Although Mum and Granny were concerned about the space, Dad was unwavering, convinced that a personal and intimate setting was the way to go.

As was the norm in such a bustling household, everyone else had started their preparations, but my mother had other plans for me. While everyone was getting ready, she decided it was the perfect moment to send me to deliver Zobo to Mrs Sanni, who lived a few blocks away. When I returned home, the compound was teeming with aunts and cousins, creating a delightful cacophony and the rich aroma of fried meat and chicken filled the air, mingling with their laughter.

As I walked through the gate, I noticed Mum leap from her chair, only to settle back down sheepishly when she realised it was just me. Aunt Oladunni, affectionately known as Aunty Dunni, stood nearby and greeted me with a smile as I made my way past her toward the house.

I figured it was best to slip away before Mum could find another task for me, with a slight grumble, I ducked back outside, hoping for a brief respite before the day's whirlwind began in earnest. As I stepped out through the side door, there was Dad, perfectly relaxed in his favourite spot on the veranda. Sipping his favourite tea, with a plate of fried meat and chicken sitting contentedly beside him he was lost in the pages of a newspaper and appeared completely at ease, a stark contrast to Mum, who was caught up in a frenzy as she oversaw preparations for Kenny's wedding.

I couldn't help but smile, Dad had always been the calm in our family storm.

"Ah, Mide!" he called, spotting me and setting his paper aside. "You've done your mother's delivery?"

"Yes, Daddy," I replied, strolling over.

"Good, good," he nodded with approval. "Come and eat with me. Take what you fancy."

I grinned as I settled into the seat beside him, reaching for a piece of chicken, I savoured the tantalising flavour that exploded in my mouth as I bit into it.

"Thank you, Daddy," I beamed at him.

He nodded, a twinkle in his eye. "Today's a big day for Kenny and for all of us, make sure you're ready in time for the ceremony."

"I will, Dad," I promised, though I knew it might be ages before I could get myself sorted out with the way my mother kept sending me on errands.

Suddenly, a ruckus erupted from inside the house.

Amid muffled voices, Mum's unmistakable sigh of relief pierced through.

"Thank God!" I heard her exclaim in relief.

Intrigued, I peeked through the window, gasping as I saw Kenny standing elegantly before the mirror in her traditional bridal outfit a true vision of beauty.

Tears stung my eyes, as it dawned on me that my sister was getting married and would soon leave our home for her husband's home. Though I was happy for her, I wasn't quite ready for the impending farewell.

Stepping away from the window, I turned to my father.

"I'm going to get dressed now, Daddy."

He nodded, waving me off with a smile as I headed back to my room to prepare for the ceremony.

Just as I walked into the house, Mum appeared in front of me, holding a basket containing bottles of Zobo.

"Mide, come quickly! Hurry!" she urged. "Take these to Amaka before you start getting ready. First, drop off two bottles at Mrs Johnson's," she added, thrusting the basket into my arms. "And be quick about it; we need to prep for our guests!"

I frowned as she moved away to check on Kenny, who was deep in conversation with her friends and my older siblings. When would I ever get the chance to prepare, with Mum always finding something for me to do? Grumbling, I hoisted the basket on my shoulders and trudged out of the house.

Dr. Amaka Adetokunbo, affectionately called 'Aunty Amaka,' was my mum's best friend.

Her house was on the same street as ours, it wasn't far for me to walk, but the weight of the day pressed heavily on my shoulders.

As I strolled, I couldn't help but reflect on how this day felt entirely different. This wasn't just any day; we would welcome the in-laws, and it would mark the beginning of Kenny's journey as a wife. I dropped off Mrs Johnson's Zobo on my way, exchanging pleasantries with her husband, who wished our family well for the wedding, before hastening to the Adetokunbo home, hoping to return before the festivities kicked off.

"Good morning, Aunty!" I exclaimed as I entered their house, carefully balancing the basket.

"My darling! How lovely to see you! Oh, you brought the zobo. I told your mum to leave it until after the wedding!" Aunty Amaka said, approaching me in a vibrant Ankara kaftan, her hair tied up neatly in a turban, already prepared for the day ahead. "How are you?"

"I am very well, Aunty. Mummy asked me to drop off these bottles of Zobo for you," I replied, handing her the basket with a small smile.

"Daalu, nwa'm. This is your mum, ehh, she could have waited till after the wedding today, aren't you meant to be getting ready?" she asked with a soft laugh. "How is she? Are all the preparations going well? I know today is a busy day for you all."

I smiled. "They're going well, Aunty. Everyone's a bit stressed, but everything's coming together."

"Good to hear! Not the stress part, though. We're getting ready now. I told your mum I would help with anything she needs, but it seems she has everything under control. Your people are inside if you want to say hello." She said, pointing towards the hallway.

"Thank you, Aunty. I will say hi before I head back," I said, grateful for the chance to linger a bit longer. It was always lovely to visit the Adetokunbos; they felt like a second family.

As I walked down the hallway and up the big stairs to Labisi's room, I thought about how close our families were. The Adetokunbos were a multicultural family, like us. Aunty Amaka was Igbo, while her husband was Yoruba. They embraced their diverse backgrounds with pride. They had three children, each with a unique personality. Still, everyone knew Oluwatife, the eldest, had a special place in Aunty Amaka's heart.

He was twenty and at university in London.

When the Aunty had struggled to conceive, she and her husband had adopted Oluwatife, whom we called Tife, as a baby. He was her miracle child, and she often referred to him as *her blessing and good luck charm*.

If Oluwatife caught even a slight cold, Aunty Amaka would fall sick with worry. A year after Tife came into their lives, Aunty Amaka had gone ahead to have two more children, Demola and Labisi who was the youngest and the baby of the house.

Friendly and accommodating, Labisi had always been the kind of person you wanted as a best friend. She was loyal, kind, and generous with everything she had.

I have always loved getting her hand-me-down clothes. She gave them to me and Alaba without a second thought.

But it was Demola, the middle child, who was my favourite of all Aunty Amaka's children. At seventeen, Demola was quiet, thoughtful, and highly organised.

He was also a very kind person.

As I neared Labisi's room, I noticed her door was wide open.

Peeking inside, I wasn't surprised to see that she was sitting cross-legged on her bed, a book in her hands. Labisi loved books. She could read for hours and sometimes forgot the world around her.

Today was no different.

"Labisi," I said in a low voice, breaking into a smile when her head shot up and she screamed with excitement.

"Mide!"

Her book fell onto the bed as she jumped up and hurried over to give me a tight hug, almost knocking me over.

That was Labisi—always full of enthusiasm.

"Hey, Labisi!" I laughed, hugging her back. "Still reading, as usual? Don't you ever take a break?"

She giggled, pulling me further into her room. "You know me, Mide. I can't help it! These books are too good! But wait, let me look at you. Wow, Mide! You've grown since the last time I saw you!" She said, turning me around as she looked me up and down.

I smiled, brushing it off. "You say that every time you see me, Labisi."

She shrugged. "Well, it's true! Anyway, are you ready for the big day?"

"Of course!" I replied, sitting down on the edge of her bed. "I am so excited!"

"Yes, oh," she teased. "I'd be surprised if the whole neighbourhood didn't turn out! Your house will be packed today."

"What about you guys? Are you coming for the event?" I asked, glancing around her room. It was organised in an orderly manner, despite the stacks of books everywhere, reflecting her discipline.

"Oh, definitely. We wouldn't miss it for the world!" she said.

Then, with a mischievous grin, she whispered, "Meanwhile, your best friend just got back from school."

"Who? Demola?" I asked, my face lighting up at the mention of her older brother.

"Who else?" she laughed. "He's in his room, sulking like he always does after exams."

"I thought it was you and Tife who were around." My comment sounded more like a question than a statement.

"Nope. Oya, go and say hello before Mum starts yelling at me to get ready. I need to take a quick shower before she starts shouting!"

I laughed, knowing all too well how Aunty Amaka behaved when she had an event to attend.

Leaving her room, I headed down the hall to Demola's room.

He had just finished his first year at university, and I hadn't seen him in months. Unlike Tife, Demola had insisted on attending University here in Nigeria. I recall when he visited our house last year. He had looked all grown up in his jeans and checkered shirt. He came to share the news that he got into university. He was only seventeen, but he had looked so much older, tall and confident.

I tapped gently on his door, and a voice from inside called out. "Come in."

Pushing the door open, I found Demola sitting at his desk, his nose buried in what looked like a textbook.

"Mide!" he said, looking up and smiling. "What's up? I didn't know you were here."

"Halo! I came to drop off some zobo for your mum, and I thought I'd stop by and say hi." I said, stepping into his room. "I didn't know you were back."

"I am. I got in today," he replied, leaning back in his chair. "How are the wedding preparations going?"

"Madness!" I said, rolling my eyes. "You know how my mum can be. She's been pacing up and down all morning, worried about Kenny's dress."

Demola chuckled. "Women and clothes."

"Exactly! "You wouldn't think a few dresses would be such a big deal," I said, feeling a bit annoyed. I recalled my mum and the fuss she made moments ago because her clothes and Kenny's outfit hadn't arrived.

"I can imagine. Aunty Toke never does things halfway, does she?"

"Not at all. It can be frustrating though but thank God everything's coming together. I think it's going to be a great day." I said, feeling the excitement bubble up again. "Are you coming to the wedding?"

"Of course! I wouldn't miss it. You want your mum to have my head if I don't show up," he said with a grin.

I laughed, knowing it was true.

Mum adored Demola and treated him like one of her own.

He was her favourite of the three, and I know she harboured dreams that he would fall for and marry one of my sisters. Perhaps Alaba, because the others were older than him.

"So, how's school?" I asked, glancing at the open books scattered across his desk. "You're always studying."

"It's going well," he said, shrugging. "University is harder than I expected, but I'm managing. It's just… a lot sometimes."

"You'll be fine. "You're the smartest person I know," I said, with genuine admiration for his dedication.

"Thank you, Mide, that means a lot," he said with a slight smile.

"Well, it's true," I said.

"You're not bad yourself, you know. I'm sure you'll do great in your exams when the time comes."

"Let's hope so," I said, feeling a bit shy under his praise. "Anyway, I'll let you get back to your books. I wanted to say hello before I head back home."

"It's always nice to see you," Demola said, standing up and walking me to the door. "Tell everyone we'll be over soon for the wedding."

"I will," I said as my eyes caught sight of something on his game table.

My curious mind kicked in, and I walked over to it.

It was a stash of games. I bent to look at them, then sat down excited to look through the games., picking up a game pad, I studied it, a frown creasing my forehead as I hadn't seen this type of controller before.

"Dreamcast." He said, as though he could see through my confusion. "The control isn't much different from Nintendo. Let me show you," Demola said, his voice relaxed as he sat behind me, stretching his legs out on either side.

It wasn't the first time he was teaching me how to play a game, but this time it felt different. His closeness felt natural, but it unexpectedly made me shy in a manner I had never experienced before.

My heartbeat quickened, and I shifted my position to focus on the game, but concentrating was difficult with him sitting behind me.

Had something changed?

Perhaps, it was me becoming more aware of myself as a young woman; my body had changed significantly over the past few months. My breasts had grown a bit more, and I'd started my period just two months ago,

But now, sitting here with Demola, the excitement of 'becoming a woman' felt distant. Instead, something new was creeping in, a nervousness, an awareness of my body that I hadn't felt before.

His nearness was affecting me in ways I couldn't explain.

As if sensing my thoughts, Demola rested his chin lightly on my shoulder, sending an unexpected shiver down my spine.

It wasn't unpleasant, but it was startling, and it caused my heart to flutter.

A few boys at school had tried to tease me, touch my cheeks or send me Valentine notes and letters, but none had ever made me feel this… off-balance.

My thoughts were racing. I needed to get up, to move, to leave. My mother hadn't sent me here to spend time with Demola or to play video games. I was supposed to be delivering zobo to Aunty Amaka, not sitting here, feeling this confusing mix of emotions.

"Where's Oluwatife?" I asked suddenly, my voice sounding too loud in the quiet room. I was desperate for a change in the atmosphere, something to break the tension that was building inside me.

"He's gone to Ghana with my cousins. I thought you guys knew," Demola replied, his voice lower, calmer.

He didn't seem to notice how flustered I was, or if he did, he didn't show it.

"Oh," I mumbled, feeling even more awkward.

I wasn't uncomfortable in a bad way, but I knew I needed to leave soon. The moment felt like it was spinning out of my control, and I didn't know how to handle it.

Demola's voice broke through my thoughts again. "Are you afraid of me?" he asked suddenly. He was still looking at the TV screen, but I could feel his attention shift to me. His question hung in the air, and I didn't know how to respond.

"No," I stammered, though my voice betrayed the confusion I was feeling. I wasn't scared, not exactly. It wasn't that I didn't trust him—it was that I didn't trust myself around him in that moment.

He gently took the game controller from my hands and placed it on the floor. I watched as he picked himself up and knelt before me, turning me to face him.

His movements were slow, deliberate, as though he was giving me time to stop him if I wanted to.

"Are you sure?" he asked, his eyes searching mine, his expression soft but serious. There was a kind of intensity in his gaze that made me feel both vulnerable and safe at the same time.

My heart pounded in my chest.

"No," I whispered again, unsure of what I meant by it. I didn't understand what was happening between us, only that something had changed.

Just like that. Our faces were slowly moving closer, like we were being drawn together by some invisible force. Demola gently held my chin, his thumb brushing my cheek. My mind was racing, filled with thoughts I didn't know how to process.

Was he going to kiss, or rather were we going to kiss? The last boy who tried to kiss me at school after he gave me a valentine's card, received a punch that ended with us fighting and having to be sent to the principal's office.

It had been that serious. Now, I felt a kiss coming but I was unable to stop myself.

"Mum, has Mide Left?" Labisi's voice suddenly called out from downstairs, cutting through the moment like a clap of thunder.

I froze, my breath catching in my throat.

"Err... I don't think so. She should be upstairs," Aunty Amaka answered.

"She's here," Demola called back, his voice steady. He stood up quickly, the moment between us dissolving as if it had never happened. He moved to the corner of the room where a chair stood, piled with freshly washed clothes he'd left there.

Gently, he began folding them as if nothing had happened.

I sat there for a moment, feeling like a frightened rabbit caught in headlights. My thoughts were jumbled, and I wasn't sure how to process what had just happened or what had almost happened.

My hands were trembling slightly, and I couldn't figure out why.

I liked Demola—he'd always been kind and patient with me. But today, something had changed, and my young self didn't know how to handle it.

There was a knock on the door, and Demola called out, "Come in."

Labisi walked in with a smile, but her eyes immediately darted between me and her brother, as if she sensed something was off. "Mide, are you okay?" she asked, her tone was light but laced with concern.

I forced a smile, trying my best to act normal. "Yes, I'm fine," I said quickly, though the words felt heavy on my tongue. "I should be going. I don't want to get in trouble with Mummy."

"Are you sure you're alright?" she pressed, her eyes narrowing slightly as if she could see right through my facade.

Why was she asking me that?

"Yes," I said again, standing up too quickly, nearly knocking over the tray of games. "I'm fine."

"Okay, let's go over to your house together then," she said, watching me closely.

"No!" I blurted out, louder than I intended.

Both Demola and Labisi stared at me in surprise. I quickly backtracked. "I mean, yes, sure, let's do that," I added, trying to sound more composed.

But inside, I was a mess.

The way I had reacted made me feel embarrassed. I could tell by the way they exchanged glances that they knew something was off.

Demola didn't say much. He just kept folding his clothes, his face neutral, though I couldn't help but wonder what he was thinking. His calmness made me even more nervous.

"See you later, Mide," he said, as I reached the door. His voice was gentle, but it sent a ripple through me that I couldn't explain.

I paused for a moment, my hand on the door handle, then quickly stepped out, with Labisi following behind me. For the first time in my life, Demola had made me feel something I didn't understand—and it excited me.

Chapter Four

The wedding celebration was in full swing, and the entire compound was buzzing with energy by the time Labisi, and I joined the family. Everywhere I looked, people were dancing, laughing, and eating. Nigerians can eat! We love our food, and no event is complete without plenty of it. My sisters and I looked stunning in our lace skirts and blouses; the tailor had taken extra care in stitching stones onto the fabrics. Even though we were young, there was something lovely about wearing our outfits; it made us feel we were part of something bigger, a family tradition, a connection to our roots.

My father stood tall and proud in his native attire.

His long, embroidered white blouse and the deep blue wrapper tied around his waist made him look regal. The coral beads around his neck and wrists added a touch of royalty, and he moved with the dignity that came with being the father of the bride. My Mum was a vision in her deep blue double wrapper and white lace blouse, with a matching head tie wrapped elegantly around her head. She also wore coral beads, and together, they looked like a king and queen presiding over the festivities.

Trust my mum to play the role of the perfect hostess; she had to, or else how would you know she was the mother of the bride? The *alaga iduro*—the lively master of ceremonies, too, was in full swing.

Her voice cut through the noise as she demanded money for every little thing, like a conductor, orchestrating the entire engagement ceremony with humour and authority. Her counterpart, the *alaga ijoko*, who represented the groom's family, was constantly begging for leniency as the playful back-and-forth continued.

It was all part of the fun, and the guests laughed along as the *alaga iduro* made it increasingly difficult for the groom's family to claim their bride. The best part, though, was when my aunties covered Kenny's friends and my older sisters with a large cloth, parading them one by one in front of Segun, the groom. Each time, Segun had to guess if the woman before him was his bride, and if he guessed wrong, he would have to pay a small fee as a penalty.

Aunty Dunni leaned over to explain the tradition to us, her eyes twinkling with mischief; "If he picks the wrong girl, it'll cost him," she whispered, grinning. "But don't worry, the money usually goes back to the family."

I laughed, enjoying the theatrics of it all.

Even though I didn't know all the rules of the tradition, I was utterly absorbed in the drama of the moment.

Just as I was about to ask my Aunty another question, I heard a squeal from beside me.

"Demo is here!" Labisi exclaimed, pointing toward the entrance.

I looked up and towards the gate to see her brother strolling into the compound, looking handsome in his crisp white buba and shokoto, a native top and trousers worn by Yoruba men in Nigeria.

I found myself staring, wondering when my childhood friend had become a handsome young man. My mind raced as I remembered what had nearly happened between us in his room; would we have kissed if Labisi hadn't entered? To my shock, I realised how much things had changed between us. I couldn't just climb all over him like I used to when we were younger. Back then, I would jump on his back or tug at his arm without a second thought.

As a child, I wanted to go everywhere Demola went.

"We kept a seat for you," Labisi's voice broke through my thoughts as she waved him over.

I watched as Demola made his way over, his smile warm and familiar. "Thanks," he said, sitting down between us. He turned to me, and I felt my heart skip for some funny reason. "Mide, you look nice," he said.

"Thank you," I mumbled, not daring to meet his eyes. My voice felt small, and I could feel my face heating up. Why was I suddenly feeling this way? It was just Demola, after all.

"And what about me?" Labisi teased, poking her brother in the side.

He laughed, giving her a playful nudge. "You look great, too."

I glanced at them, noticing how effortlessly they bantered with each other. I didn't know why, but something tightened in my chest as I watched them. It was a strange feeling—like a knot that I couldn't quite put into words.

I stood up abruptly, desperate for an excuse to leave.

"I'll bring you some food," I said quickly, not waiting for a response.

"I'll come with you," Demola offered, half-rising from his seat.

"No!" I said, a little too quickly. "I mean, no, it's fine. I can manage."

Labisi, with her eagle eyes, sensed something because she gently tugged at Demola's sleeve, pulling him back into his seat. "Let her go. She's got it covered."

I hurried toward the kitchen, my heart still racing from the unexpected surge of emotions. I didn't want Demola to mention anything about what had happened in his room earlier, and the thought of being alone with him again made me nervous. As soon as I entered the kitchen, I saw Aunty Dunni bustling around, organising the trays of food.

"Aunty, I need to get some food for Demola," I said, my voice shaky.

Aunty Dunni raised an eyebrow, a mischievous grin spreading across her face. "Ah, so you're bringing food for your husband now, eh?"

I nearly dropped the plate I was holding. "My what? Aunty, stop it."

"Ehn, wedding bells will be ringing soon for both of you, abi?" she teased, winking at Taiye, who had just walked in from the doorway.

"Oooh, stop it!" I muttered, feeling the heat rise to my cheeks.

Taiye joined in, laughing as she added, "But isn't he your husband, *Mide*? You two have been inseparable since you were kids. You didn't mind when we called you his wife back then."

"Well, I mind now." I spat out.

"Aah…okay oh. Sorry, oh." Taiye said, laughing mischievously.

Aunty Dunni decided to pick up from where she left off. "But you both…"

"Aunty, please stop," I interrupted, looking at her with both hands open. I felt thoroughly embarrassed. Why was everyone teasing me today?

"Okay, okay," Aunty Dunni relented, handing me a plate of jollof rice, salad, plantain and peppered chicken. "Here you go. Now, go feed your 'friend.'"

I rolled my eyes, grateful that she didn't push the joke any further. Grabbing the plate, I made my way back to where Demola and Labisi were seated. The music from the live band had picked up, and the lively beats filled the air as I crossed the courtyard.

When I reached them, Demola smiled as I handed him the plate. "Thanks, Mide."

I nodded, still avoiding his gaze. "You're welcome."

Today felt like the strangest day of my life.

Between the excitement of the wedding and the teasing from my family, everything felt like it was changing, and I didn't know how to handle it. I watched him from the corner of my eye, still trying to make sense of the emotions swirling inside me. Each time he caught my eye, he smiled, making my heart skip a beat.

Maybe things really were changing—both for him and for me.

* * *

I was happy when the celebration finally came to an end, but then I realised it was time for Kenny to leave for her new home. The mood had moved from the lively excitement of the wedding to a quieter, more intimate atmosphere. As my mum's favourite daughter, Kenny's departure from our house felt significant.

I sniffled a little as my Mum suddenly started crying.

Dad, as usual, was there to console her, but we could see he was also emotional. There was a lingering sense of finality as realised Kenny, was not going to be living with us any longer.

"Kenny, are you ready?" Taiye asked, holding onto one of Kenny's bags as we all hovered by the doorway.

Kenny, dressed in a simple and elegant attire, nodded, looking at our mother, who was trying to gather herself and then continue her fussing over Kenny. "I think so," she said slowly, glancing around the house as though soaking it all in for the last time.

"You'll be fine," I reassured her with a small smile, even though I had no idea what I was talking about. I could sense that she was nervous, even if she wasn't saying it out loud.

Mum stepped forward, adjusting Kenny's gele one last time.

My sister looked gorgeous in her going-away outfit, which was a combination of green aso oke and purple and green lace.

"Remember everything we talked about, and don't forget to call me if you need anything," Mum said, her voice full of emotion. She had stopped crying, but we all knew she was trying hard not to.

It was hard for her to watch Kenny move into this new phase of life.

Kenny smiled gently, nodding again. "I will, Mum."

With that, we all headed out, Taiye, Alaba, and I walking alongside Kenny as we climbed into the car that would take her to her in-laws. The drive was quiet, a stark contrast to the earlier festivities' bustling energy.

I sat beside Kenny, holding her hand, trying to offer her some silent support.

My sister had left our mother's nest.

Now I felt so alone.

* * *

When we arrived at her new home, Kenny's in-laws greeted us warmly, welcoming their new daughter-in-law. We spent the night with her, helping her settle in.

There was a subtle sadness in the air, but we did our best to concentrate on the happiness of the occasion. Kenny's mother-in-law was one of the first to greet us when we arrived. There was something in her smile that made me uneasy; it wasn't the same smile she had flashed just a few hours earlier at the wedding.

I just hoped I was overthinking things and there was nothing to worry about.

The next morning, we said our goodbyes, cried with Kenny, hugged her, and then we headed back home.

The house felt different without her; there was a gap, a sense that something significant had changed. Daddy allowed me to move into Kenny's room, much to Mum's irritation. There were still plenty of visits from family and friends, keeping the house lively in the days after Kenny's wedding. I was pleased to have my own room and spent the rest of the holiday reading and preparing for school.

I came up with reasons to avoid going to Labisi's house. I couldn't bring myself to face Demola, not after everything I'd been feeling during the wedding. The tension, the confusion—it was all too much, and I wasn't ready to deal with it.

Whenever the Adetokunbos visited us, I would quietly slip away, pretending to be busy with something else. It became my way of coping, and before I knew it, the holiday days blurred together and flew past.

The start of the new school term arrived sooner than expected, bringing with it the rush of returning to lessons, assignments, and the usual bustle of high school life. I hadn't seen Demola since the wedding, but I learned from Labisi that he had spent the rest of his holiday with Tife and their cousins in Ghana. I was somewhat relieved that I wouldn't have to see him and face the feelings I had been avoiding.

CHAPTER FIVE

Before I knew it, two years had passed like that, and I was in SS2, when I saw Demola again. I had thought about him occasionally over those two years, wondering how he was doing, but I never reached out.

Demola was in his third year at university when we saw each other again, and it wasn't how I had imagined we'd meet, though.

I had imagined it differently—perhaps a chance meeting during one of his visits home or maybe crossing paths at a family gathering, but that was not how it turned out.

It was a regular school day when I received the news from one of my classmates about Demola.

Moji Oshodi also knew the Adetokunbo family.

She approached me during lunch break, a smirk on her face. We all knew Moji as a community town crier. There was nothing she didn't know about everything.

"Mide, how far? Did you hear Demola's back from school?" she asked as she popped a sweet into her mouth.

My breath caught in my chest at the mention of his name, but I kept a calm demeanour. "Oh, really? I didn't know."

"Yeah, he's back…" Moji hesitated, her face suddenly serious with a parrot-like look. "I heard he was in an accident."

The words hung in the air, and a chill ran down my spine. "An accident?" I repeated, my voice sounding far away.

"Yeah. I heard he's okay now, but it wasn't good. He had to take some time off school to recover."

I stood there, frozen, my mind racing. How come I didn't know? I hadn't seen Demola in almost two years, as he had spent every holiday he had in London, and now I was hearing that he had been in an accident. The shock of it hit me harder than I expected. I realised then how much I had missed him, how much I had buried my confused feelings over the past two years.

And now, the thought of him being hurt stirred up all the emotions I had been avoiding.

After school that evening, I went straight to my mother. "Mummy, I heard Demola was in an accident," I said, trying to sound calm but not caring if she knew.

Mum nodded, her expression turning serious. "Yes, Amaka told me. But don't worry, he's recovering well. He will be fine."

"How come no one said anything?" I asked because I really wanted to know why I was only hearing about it now, and from an outsider, that hurt.

"Because he only just rang his mum yesterday and told her. No one knew my dear."

No one knew? So how did Moji know?

I nodded, but the worry still gnawed at me. I wanted to see him, to make sure he was okay with my own eyes. But I didn't know if I could face him after all this time, especially after the confusing feelings I had tried so hard to suppress.

It wasn't until the following week that I finally gathered the courage to visit the Adetokunbos. As I walked up to their house, my heart pounded in my chest as I wasn't sure what to expect.

Would he be the same Demola I had grown up with, or would things be different now? Would I still feel the same way I had during Kenny's wedding? Would he even let me into the house to see him, considering I knew about his situation and had chosen to stay away?

The thoughts were killing me.

When I knocked on the door, it was Labisi who answered, her face lighting up when she saw me.

"Mide! It's been so long! I haven't seen you since Christmas! Ha, are you avoiding us?" she exclaimed, pulling me into a hug.

"I know, I would have come earlier, I am sorry for not calling when I heard you had come back home from Uni," I said, smiling, though my thoughts were elsewhere.

"It's cool—no need to explain." She said smiling. I rang your house this morning to ask after you.

"That's nice…How's Demola?"

"He's doing much better, he'll live. He's inside. Do you want to see him?"

I hesitated for a moment but then nodded. Was she serious? Of course, I wanted to see him. "Yes, I do."

As I stepped inside, my heart raced with anticipation. It had been almost two years since I had last seen him, and the memory of that wedding day, and all the confusing emotions that came with it, came flooding back.

But then I wasn't thirteen anymore.

When I finally saw him, sitting in the living room with his leg propped up, a wave of relief washed over me. He looked tired but still had that same easy smile I remembered. Two years had made a difference in his appearance, though. Demola looked like he'd been living in a gym. His arms and shoulders were nicely sculpted, and I could see his strong abs through his t-shirt.

My eyes rolled over to his shorts and stayed there.

"Hey, Mide," he said, his eyes meeting mine. "It's been a while."

"Yes, it has," I said slowly, my voice sounded more like a squeak. I swallowed hard then tried to smile.

Everything felt different—and yet, somehow the same. I didn't move. I stood there in the living room, taking in the sight of Demola, and I felt a strange mix of emotions. Seeing him now brought back a flood of memories. His eyes were the same warm brown, and his smile had that familiar, easy charm, but there was a weariness about him now. He was more grown-up, not just physically, but in the way he carried himself, more thoughtful, more reserved.

"Come sit down," Demola said, gesturing to the couch beside him. He adjusted his position slightly, wincing as he moved his injured leg. "I'm not going anywhere anytime soon," he added with a chuckle as he watched my face.

Was I that obvious? I sat down, my heart still racing from seeing him again. "I heard about the accident," I said quietly. "I'm glad you're okay."

"Thank you," he replied, looking down at his leg. "It was rough for a while," But I'm getting better."

"What about school?" I asked innocently.

"You're so cute." He said, making me blush. "I had to take some time off from school, but I'm almost back to normal now." He smiled again, though I could see the shadow of frustration in his eyes.

"Demo, why didn't you tell me?" I asked, sounding frustrated with him.

"Mide. I haven't seen you in almost two years, yet you live just a couple of minutes away from me, you never bothered to look for me, though I came round to yours to check on you a couple of times."

We sat in silence for a moment, the weight of his words hanging between us.

I wasn't sure of what to say next. The last time I had seen Demola, everything had felt confusing, and I hadn't been able to process the changes happening between us. And now, here he was, sitting right next to me, and I still didn't know what to make of it.

"Two years is a long time, Mide," he said, breaking the silence. "I missed seeing you around."

I looked at him, surprised by his honesty. "I missed you too," I admitted, my voice softer than I intended. It was the truth, but I hadn't allowed myself to think about it until now.

Was our relationship weird?

He shifted slightly, turning to face me more directly. "So why didn't you visit?" he asked, his tone gentle but curious. "I mean, Labisi thought you were avoiding us. Did I do something wrong?"

I froze for a second, unsure of how to answer.

It wasn't that he had done something wrong, but how could I explain the swirl of emotions that had taken over me during the wedding? How could I tell him that I had felt something change between us, and it had scared me?

"I wasn't avoiding coming around," I said, though even I knew that wasn't entirely true. "I just. I don't know. Things have been tough lately."

He tilted his head slightly, studying me. "Why? What happened?"

I took a deep breath, trying to find the right words. "I don't know. Things seem different to me these days, even you. You look, I don't know… different. Everything feels strange, like something has changed within me, and I don't know what to do with that. Am I even making sense to you, Demo?"

For a moment, I couldn't believe I had just said all of that out loud.

My cheeks flushed with embarrassment, hoping he wouldn't catch on.

I quickly looked down at my hands, which were nervously fidgeting in my lap.

Demola was silent for a moment, taking in what I'd said. Then he let out a soft sigh, a gentle smile playing on his lips. "You aren't the only one who notices things changing," he said, his voice low. "Here, school, you, me. There are changes everywhere, Mide. It's because we are growing older."

I looked up, startled by his response. "You…?" That was the only part I heard.

He nodded, leaning back against the sofa. "Yeah, I did. I don't know exactly when these things happen, but I understand growing up is a part of it. I mean, look at you, I used to see you just as the kid who followed me around everywhere, but suddenly you weren't; you aren't a kid anymore, Mide."

His words echoed my own thoughts, and I felt a sense of relief wash over me.

"I guess I didn't know how to deal with it," I admitted. "I didn't know if I should just pretend everything was the same or if it was okay to acknowledge that things were different."

Demola chuckled softly, his eyes crinkling at the corners. "Yeah, I get that. It happens to all of us."

We both fell into a comfortable silence, the tension from earlier slowly fading away. It felt good to talk about things, to acknowledge that things had changed but that we were still us.

"So," he said after a while, his tone lighter, "are we good now? Can I stop worrying that I somehow scared you off?"

I laughed, shaking my head. "Yes, we're fine. And no, no one scared me off. I think I scared myself off."

He grinned, and for a moment, it felt like we were back to our old selves, just Demola and Mide, the way we used to be, before everything got complicated.

"Good," he said, leaning back with a satisfied sigh. "Because I'm stuck at home for a while, and I'll need someone to keep me company while I'm recovering."

I raised an eyebrow, grinning at him, "You mean you need someone to play video games with you?"

"Well, that too," he admitted with a laugh. "But seriously, it'd be nice to hang out again. It's just you, Tife and mum who seem to have my time."

I smiled, feeling a warmth spread through me. "Yeah, I'd like that."

We sat together talking more about our schools while he had his dinner.

The weight that had been hanging over me for the past two years gradually lifted. Soon it was time for me to go home. I said goodbye to Demola, and he pulled me into a hug as usual.

As I hugged him, I knew in my heart that things were different. I was slowly losing my brother Demola. My feelings for him had changed into something not so brotherly. I closed my eyes, reminding myself that although things were different, different didn't have to mean bad.

I couldn't talk with my mum like I did with Demola, so being able to do that was a blessing.

CHAPTER SIX

I spent the next couple of weeks with Demola, and I must admit that it was the best part of my life. After school every day, I would head to his house, where we would play video games and chat into the night. To my surprise, my mother didn't bother about me; she was too busy worrying about Kenny, who had just suffered another loss.

A miscarriage.

Her first pregnancy had resulted in a stillbirth.

I couldn't imagine the pain Kenny must be feeling; I had a feeling thing weren't going well with Kenny in her new home. There was a bit of tension between her and her mother-in-law, something I had sensed from the very beginning.

I remembered Granny saying the same thing when Segun's family came for the introduction.

"Something about this family doesn't sit well with me." She had told us, after Segun left with his family, the first time they came to visit.

"Mama, what is it again?" my mum had countered. "What is wrong with the family?"

"I don't know, but I feel there is something not right, especially with the mother."

That comment had resulted in a heated argument with mum, saying Granny did not wish her well because she didn't have a son. I remember looking at my mum, wondering what she was talking about.

There was nothing wrong with what Granny had said.

I like my sister's husband, but I have always had reservations about him. He was kind, yes, but weak. He still lived with his parents, something I could never quite understand. It wasn't very common in Nigeria. Parents could visit their children, and they might end up living with them for reasons best known to them, but it was rare for a man to marry and move into his parents' house with his wife. From everything I had heard and seen, their home was anything but comfortable, to say the least. Segun's mother was a different kind of trouble. The first time Alaba and I visited Kenny after the wedding, his mother was insistent on everyone kneeling to greet her. She placed an unhealthy importance on her idea of 'tradition'. Every small detail mattered to her, the kind of things most people didn't even notice. The last two years had given me reason to dislike her more, and I know that Kenny is trapped in a house that feels suffocating. I felt sorry for her. Alaba and I often joked that if either of us married into that family, we wouldn't have lasted three months. We would have shown Segun's mother "pepper," as they say, but maybe that would have only made things worse. Still, the thought of our bold defiance brought a small smile to my face.

Kenny wasn't like us. She was patient, perhaps even too patient.

Thank goodness, Mummy was coming home with Kenny in a few days so she could rest a bit. For us, that was good news considering no one enjoyed visiting her at her in-laws. It wasn't because we didn't like brother Segun. I still thought he was a good man, just not strong enough to stand up to his family.

I had started taking extra lessons outside our house the year before my final year in secondary school. Mummy wasn't a fan of the idea, as I had to walk quite a distance to get to the venue, where the lessons were held, but Daddy thought it was perfectly fine for me to learn alongside other students.

He thought Mummy was being overprotective.

He'd always been more relaxed, more trusting of our independence and often asked my mother, "What harm could there possibly be in letting her learn with others?"

And so, my Mum had agreed, to allow me to go for lessons in an Educational Centre, three streets away from ours. Knowing how paranoid my Mum was, I always made sure I was home early from lessons except on the days Teacher Okafor kept us for an extra twenty minutes.

Today was one of those days when lessons had run late, and I was in a hurry to get home. The estate was quiet, which was surprising; normally, it was always busy, with workers milling about and a few hawkers permitted to enter the estate. The air felt too still, like the moment just before a downpour, though the sky was clear.

I had just passed one of the buildings under construction, not paying it much attention, when I noticed a strange woman standing in front of one of the uncompleted buildings on the estate. She looked unkempt, or more like she had been robbed and beaten. Her clothes were dishevelled, and her hair was a mess. The woman looked as if she had been through something terrible. I wondered if she had been robbed or maybe beaten. There was something about her that made me hesitate, but my instinct to help kicked in.

I walked up to her.

"Are you okay, ma?" I called out, taking a few steps toward her.

She didn't reply.

Her eyes locked onto mine, and for a brief second, I thought I saw relief in them. "I need help," she said, her voice shaky.

Common sense told me to walk away and seek help for her, but as I said, my desire to help drove me to approach her. I moved closer, my heart pounding as I prepared to offer whatever assistance I could.

But before I could say another word, someone grabbed me from behind, a firm hand covered my mouth, muffling my scream, while another arm wrapped around my waist, lifting me off the ground. My mind raced in panic as I realised it was a man's hand.

I struggled to free myself, but it was of no use. The person holding me was far stronger than I was. I was a tall girl, and although I wasn't thin, my strength didn't compare to his. The coarse fabric muffled my screams, pushed against my face as I was dragged into the half-finished building, my feet scraping the dirt as I fought to free myself.

At some point, I caught the eye of the woman who had called for help.

She didn't help me but stood watching the whole scene unfold.

The fear that had been visible in her eyes earlier had disappeared, and it was replaced by pure determination. Her jaw had tightened, shoulders squared, and whatever had shaken her before was gone — or at least buried beneath something colder, harder.

"Oya, give me my money and let me go," she said, looking away from me.

Whatever was in the handkerchief pressed against my mouth and nose made me feel dizzy.

My vision blurred, and my strength faded with every second. I tried to scream again, to kick, but my body felt as if it was slipping away, growing weaker.

The darkness surrounded me, and then there was nothing.

I woke up with a throbbing headache, trying to focus on my surroundings, and felt the weight of someone pressing down on me, holding me down when I tried to move.

Panic flared in my chest.

The room was dim, just enough light to make out the shape hovering over me, a silhouette too still to be natural. I couldn't see his face, only the outline of a shoulder, the glint of something metallic near his wrist.

"Sweet girl, don't move," a voice whispered, close to my ear. Calm and controlled.

His voice was low and sinister, sending shivers down my spine. I tried to push him off me, but I was too weak to do so. My mind raced, desperate for a way out. I pushed at him, but my arms were weak and becoming increasingly powerless. I was trembling and too disoriented, too dizzy to focus clearly on anything. In a surge of panic, I scratched his skin repeatedly, desperately trying to defend myself.

He reacted by hitting me, hard, then he proceeded to grab my hands with the help of another person. Together, they pinned my hands above my head. My mind started to shut down, retreating into numbness, but the pain spread through my body, sharp and unbearable as I felt something thick ram between my legs causing me to scream out in pain. I couldn't bear it any longer. I closed my eyes, wishing I could escape, willing myself to be anywhere but here.

Maybe if I stopped fighting, the pain would stop.

I don't remember what happened next, but I felt my body go limp from the pain. And then, just like that, everything faded to black again, and I slipped back into unconsciousness.

* * *

I was alone when I finally regained consciousness. I was lying by myself in a cold, empty building. I could feel the silence as if it was heavy and pressing in from all sides.

I felt cold, dirty, sweaty and thirsty.

My head throbbed with unrelenting pain, and the dull ache in my face served as a reminder of the blows I had taken. My face pulsated, and I could taste the blood in my mouth. The darkness felt like an enemy to me, so I simply curled up and wept. I lay on the old floor, trembling, every part of me aching as I tried to understand where I was. I sobbed silently, curling into myself, feeling as if the darkness itself had turned against me.

I felt an intense pain between my thighs when I tried to move.

Wincing, I sat up, moaning in pain. I looked down, eyes widening as I saw the blood between my thighs. It was smeared on my thighs, staining my skin, confirming what I suspected had happened to me.

I froze as I realised, I had been raped.

Tears blurred my vision, but I couldn't stop them this time as they ran freely down my face, burning my cheeks as I tried to come to terms with what had been done to me. I struggled to sit up and reach for my clothes on the floor, but the movement brought a fresh wave of agony. My shirt was torn, barely held together at the seams, but my jeans were intact, as was my underwear. I gently put them on.

Each movement was slow and painful.

My whole body was screaming with pain, my entire body hurt.

How could something like this have happened to me?

Gradually, I forced myself to stand, but my legs nearly gave way beneath me. I had to steady myself on the wall to prevent myself from collapsing again. The pain was excruciating, and I wept as I limped towards the doorway, every step feeling like I was dragging my entire body through a field of needles.

The only thing that mattered to me now was getting home safe and sound.

Thankfully, my parents weren't home when I got back.

The house was quiet as I let myself in.

I quickly slipped the key into the kitchen door lock and said a small prayer of thanksgiving for not losing my keys. My hands trembled as I turned the lock, the weight of what had just happened pressing down on me like a boulder.

As I walked through the kitchen, I heard Alaba's voice call out from the living room. "Mide, is that you?"

I froze. "Yes, I just got back." My voice was muffled as I pressed both palms against my face, trying to calm my breathing and trying to manage the pain.

"Okay," she replied casually and continued watching TV.

Relief washed over me in that moment, as I had no idea what I would say if she came to the door and saw me. I wasn't ready to explain what had happened to her.

Would I ever be ready?

Quietly, I made my way to my room, shutting the door behind me as gently as I could. The second I was alone, I collapsed onto the floor, tears threatening to spill again, but I forced them back.

I couldn't let myself break down.

Not now.

I had to take a shower. I felt dirty; all of me felt dirty.

I stumbled into the bathroom, determined to wash off the stench of what had happened to me. Standing under the knob, I let the hot water run over me as I sank to the floor of the shower and had a good cry.

Tears of anger ran down my cheeks as I scrubbed and scrubbed until my fair skin was raw with red patches blooming across my arms and legs.

But it wasn't enough.

Nothing felt clean.

I couldn't remember how long I sat there, curled up as the water cascaded over me, washing away the blood and grime but doing nothing to erase the trauma.

I had been raped.

Standing before the mirror a few minutes later, I examined my bruises; my body was covered in red patches where I had been manhandled, the right side of my face was red, and I had a swollen lip.

Suddenly, the pain within me was replaced with anger.

Anger at the world for producing animals like the man, or was it men, that had raped me.

Anger at myself for being so foolish and trusting despite everything I had been taught, but all the anger in the world couldn't change the fact that I had been raped.

* * *

I must have dozed off because I woke up to the sound of Alaba knocking on my door.

"Are you sleeping?" she asked as she came towards my bed.

"Huh?" I blinked, disoriented, my limbs had gone stiff and cold from sitting in the bath for too long.

My eyes met Alaba's as I sat up in my bed.

"What happened?" she screamed, her eyes widening as they took in my bruised face, my swollen lips, the cuts and scratches that marred my smooth face.

My heart raced.

I had to come up with something believable before she ran to alert whoever was in the house. "I—uh—I was trying to leave the building after lessons, and then NEPA took the light." I swallowed hard, my throat burning from the lie. "I stumbled and fell."

"Gosh, Mide! Does it hurt?" she asked, her voice thick with concern as she stepped closer, touching my face while her eyes scanned it.

"Like hell," I admitted, trying to force a weak smile. "But I'm fine, Alaba. Thank God I didn't burst my eyes, right?" I tried to joke through the pain. I even let out a laugh, which was forced and shaky, feeling like a betrayal of the pain I was truly experiencing, but I had no choice.

Alaba couldn't know what had happened to me.

No one could know.

She let out a small laugh, but I could see the worry written all over her face. "You're so lucky. Imagine if you had really hurt your eyes," she said, shaking her head.

"I know," I responded. Still trying to make light of the situation.

"Hmmm. It would have been terrible, oh. Let me get some paracetamol from the cupboard. I'll be right back."

As she hurried out of the room, I slowly swung my feet over the side of the bed. I just needed to get through the rest of the evening without breaking down.

When Alaba returned with the pills, I forced another smile as she handed me a glass of water. "Here," she said gently, "Take these, it should help with the pain."

"Thanks," I murmured, taking the pills from her and swallowing them.

It wasn't easy ignoring the ache that still radiated through my body. I just wanted to sleep, to escape from the nightmare that had become my reality.

"Are you sure you are, okay?" Alaba asked again, her voice filled with concern as she hovered near the door.

"I'm fine," I insisted, my voice firmer this time. "I'll be okay. I just need to rest."

She nodded, but I could see that she didn't entirely believe me. "Okay," she said finally. "Get some sleep. I'll tell Daddy you're not feeling well, so no one bothers you."

"Thank you, but please don't tell him I hurt myself. You know he will start to worry," I pleaded with her.

"So how are you going to hide this?"

"I'll find a way, Alaba."

She looked at me for a moment, then nodded and mumbled, "Okay."

"Thank you," I whispered, grateful for her kindness, even though it made me feel even guiltier for hiding the truth from her.

As soon as she left, I curled up on my bed, pulling the blanket over myself as tightly as I could, as if it could shield me from everything that had happened.

No number of blankets or showers could wash away the shame and fear that plagued my aching body.

The pain remained, both physical and emotional, and I felt hollow inside.

All I could do was pray that tomorrow would be better and that I would somehow find a way to get through it.

I went to sleep hoping that the nightmare wouldn't follow me there.

It did.

Chapter Seven

The next day wasn't any better.

I woke up shaking as images of the attack flooded my memory. Sitting up in my bed, I hugged my knees to my chest and cried like a baby.

How could I have been so stupid?

Today was Friday, and I had promised Demola I would visit and keep him company. But I couldn't go to his house like this; I was too ashamed even to leave my room.

Thankfully, Alaba had kept everyone away from my door, and for that, I was grateful. I waited until I was sure the house had emptied for the day before I got up, cleaned myself for the second time that morning, and got dressed, draping a scarf around my face to hide the bruises.

I stepped out, praying my grandmother wouldn't be in the kitchen.

Luck was on my side. I slipped out of the house and onto our quiet street. I needed the fresh air to clear my head—and I needed to visit the pharmacy.

This morning, when I tried to pee, a sharp, burning pain shot through me, radiating up to my abdomen. I knew I needed to get something for it. I couldn't talk to Alaba, and I couldn't tell my mum—she'd kill me before I even had the chance to explain what had happened.

As I walked down the road, struggling not to cry, I suddenly realized I didn't even know how I had ended up heading toward Demola's house.

Before I could stop myself, I pressed the doorbell.

The door opened, and there was Demola, leaning on his walking stick.

"Mide?" It was more of a question than a statement.

I said nothing and just pulled down the headscarf covering my face.

The shock on his face had me wincing as I looked down, the tears filled my eyes.

"Demola, who is it?" a voice interrupted, from behind him.

Demola hurriedly pulled my scarf around my face, pulling me into the house to close the door behind me.

"My friend Mide, Mide, meet Ify my friend from Uni."

"Hi Ify." I struggled to whisper as my mouth still hurt to talk.

"Your friend?" Ify repeated, ignoring me, the disdain in her voice barely concealed. She looked me over, sizing me up as though I were something unpleasant she'd stepped on. "Hi." She finally said, but there was no warmth in her tone.

"Hello," I repeated quietly, trying to hide my discomfort. I quickly turned my attention back to Demola. "Demola, can I talk to you?"

His brows furrowed with concern. "Sure. Are you okay?"

"Yes." But my voice was weak, betraying me.

"Demola nodded slowly, frowning as he nodded towards his room, "Wait in my room, Ify was just leaving, let me see her out."

I nodded, not bothering to glance at Ify, I turned and walked towards Demola's room, I had barely sat down when he walked back into his room and closed the door.

As soon as I saw him, I broke down in tears.

Demola rushed to me and grabbed me in a tight but comforting hug.

"Shhh...Mide what is it? Please tell me. What happened to you?" Concern was evident in his voice. He kept comforting me until I stopped crying. "Can you talk now?" he asked.

I looked down at the floor, my heart thudding in my chest. How could I say this?

How could I tell Demola I had been raped.

I'd played this moment in my mind repeatedly, but now that it was real, the words seemed stuck. After what felt like forever, I finally forced the words out.

"It wasn't my fault." I started to say in a muffled tone.

"What wasn't your fault and what happened to you?" Demola asked, pulling the scarf away to study my bruised face. "Mide, who did this to you?"

"I may have contracted an STD, I don't know, it hurts when I try to pee, I was going to the pharmacy to get something for the pain, but I found myself coming here instead" I said still mumbling.

There was a long pause as Demola tried to process what I was saying.

Then his face changed, shock settling in. "Wait! Are you saying you've been… you know, active? Mide, you are just fifteen."

His words hit me like a blow.

My heart sank. Did he think…I shook my head quickly, tears welling up in my eyes.

"No, Demo… it's not like that," I said, my voice breaking.

He looked confused but softened when he saw my tears. "Then what is it, Mide? We can talk about that later, what happened to you, were you in a fight?" he asked gently, his tone now full of concern. "Talk to me."

"I didn't do anything to deserve it." I wept.

"Did something happen at home? He asked. "You are not making any sense. What…"

"I was raped Demola, on my way back from lesson yesterday, I was raped." I whispered. Demola froze; I grimaced at the look on his face. He looked as if he had lost every drop of blood in his body.

"What did you say? Mide?"

"It wasn't my fault, I swear. I tried to stop him." I said as tears continued to pour down my face as if a tap had been opened.

Demola pulled me into his arms, holding my head against his chest. "Oh my God, Mide… I'm so sorry," he whispered, his voice filled with anguish.

"I was so scared," I cried into his chest, my whole-body trembling. "I didn't know what to do. I just want to forget it ever happened, but now… now I don't know what's wrong with me."

He held me tighter, his hands gently rubbing my back as I cried. "I'm so, so sorry this happened to you. Who did this? Do you know who it was?"

"I didn't see their faces, I think they were two, Oh God, I don't even know how many men raped me."

"I'm sorry Mide. I'm so sorry."

Tears flowed freely down my cheeks as the memory flooded back—the fear, the pain, and the helplessness I felt. We stayed like that for what felt like forever, him comforting me as the weight of what I had been holding in finally came out.

His presence, his warmth, was the only thing keeping me from falling apart completely.

"Demola that's not all."

"There's more?!" He roared. "I'll find this idiot and I'll kill him."

"Demo when I tried to pee, it hurt." That got him to shut up.

"Yeah, you said so. Mide, you need to see a doctor. Wait, have you seen one?" he asked again.

"It happened yesterday, I haven't told anyone, not even my parents, I could only think of telling you."

"Mide, you need to speak to your parents"

"I can't." I said quietly.

"Okay, do you trust me Mide?" he asked quietly, holding my face so our

eyes met. I nodded, "If I didn't, I wouldn't be here Demola."

Demola looked into my eyes, his face full of concern. "We need to tell my mum, she is a doctor and then we need to speak to your parents, you can't handle this alone."

"Are you crazy?" I asked in a low whisper shaking my head immediately. Panic rising again.

My eyes widened. "No. my mum will blame me," I whispered in tears.

"Mide if you trust me, let my mother help us." Sensing my reservations, he held my shoulders, looking at me with gentle but serious eyes, he said. "Mum will help. I promise, she won't tell your parents unless you want her to."

My laugh tasted bitter in my mouth. "Are you joking?" I asked, looking at him in pure disbelief.

"No." he said. His face was serious. "Will you trust me?" he asked looking into my eyes. "Please Mide."

My brain was in battle with itself, but I knew I could. I trusted him.

"Okay," I whispered finally, barely able to say the word. "We'll talk to her."

He gave me a small, reassuring smile, squeezing my hand gently. "Everything will be fine Mide. Thank you for trusting me," he said gently, leading me to his bed. "Lie, down and wait while I get my Mum." He leaned down and kissed my forehead. "Everything will be alright Mide, trust me."

I waited till he had left the room before I burst into tears again, as I recalled the events of the previous day, how could I have been so foolish. Five minutes later, Demola came back into the room with his mum. "Good afternoon aunty." I greeted.

"Chineke! Mide what happened to you?" his Mum screamed as she saw my face. She rushed to the bed and helped me sit up, then sat on the bed beside me.

I looked at Demola and then back to her. It wasn't easy for me to narrate my ordeal to his Mum, but I knew I had to.

"Mide, do you want to talk to me alone?" Mrs Adetokunbo asked. "Is it something to do with you Demo?" her sharp eyes pinned him to the spot where he stood.

Demola looked at me and nodded, and his mother caught it.

"Demola what did you do?" She asked looking at him.

"Nothing mum. What are you asking me?" He answered still watching me, willing me to speak.

"Would one of you say something please?" aunt Amaka said. Still, we said nothing, so she looked me in the eye then asked. "Who beat you up Mide? Did Demola or someone I know do this to you?"

"No." I shouted. I noticed she let out a breath of relief.

"Mum, why would you think I would hit Mide? Seriously mum," Demola whispered in surprise.

"What? Since you both have refused to say something, what do you want me to think? Now what is going on?" Her gaze pinned us right there.

"Please calm down mum, Mide has something to say to you."

I wanted to scream at them. *I'm here. Stop talking over me.*

"Mide, please tell me who did this to you." Aunty Amaka repeated slowly.

That wasn't a question I could answer easily.

It brought back painful memories of my attack and those memories always led to tears, which was exactly what happened there.

The dam broke and I lost my composure.

I must have shocked aunt Amaka because she immediately enveloped me in a hug and let me cry. Meanwhile, she kept opening her hands to her son, asking what was going on, but he signalled that she wait for me. The comfort I got from this woman was one I knew I could never get from my own mother, so I was grateful I had her at that moment. Minutes later when I had stopped crying, she offered me food, but I told her I had eaten.

It was Demola who touched my shoulder and told me to talk to his mum.

He offered to leave but I insisted he stayed so he sat on the other side of me and held my hand.

Aunty Amaka watched us throughout.

There was something I didn't understand about the way she looked at us then, but it was comforting.

"Talk to me my darling." She said still holding my hand.

"Can you promise not to tell my parents?" I asked her.

"I have to know what this is about before…"

"You have to promise mum." Demola interrupted. He was pleading with her with his eyes.

"Hmmm…I hope I do not regret this." She spoke. "Now tell me. What is going on?"

I took a deep breath and uttered the words that I didn't want to say. "Aunty, yesterday, on my way back from lesson, I was raped."

The shock on Aunt Amaka's face tore at me, and my eyes filled with tears as she gathered me into her arms and rocked me back and forth while I cried.

After I had cried my heart out, she made jollof rice and dodo and ensured I ate before taking me to the hospital for an examination. At the hospital, after I had been examined and prescribed antibiotics, Aunty Amaka turned to me and said quietly, "We are going home to speak to your parents. I know it's hard to believe me right now, but you will get through this," Aunty Amaka said, her voice soft but filled with conviction.

I looked at her, not entirely sure if I believed her as my eyes filled with tears.

"You're stronger than you realise, Mide" she continued, leaning forward, her eyes locking with mine. "The scars, both inside and out, they'll never fully fade. But that doesn't mean they define you. What defines you is your resilience, your ability to rise, even when it feels impossible."

I felt something move inside me as she spoke, as if her words were lifting a small part of the weight I carried. She smiled then, a knowing smile, the kind that told me she understood everything I hadn't yet put into words.

"You're not alone," Demola said from beside me, reaching out to gently squeeze my hand. "Support is a strong thing, and you've got an incredible one. You'll do well, my dear. I know it. Talk to someone when you feel you need to. Recognise you have a strong support system and don't take it for granted."

CHAPTER EIGHT

When we got to our house, I hesitated at the doorway, before I took a deep breath and walked into my home. Every step I took behind Aunty Amaka and Demola felt heavier than the last. Slowly, I followed Demola and his Mum, my chest tightened as the living room came into view.

My parents sat close together, voices low as they chatted with Granny.

The moment I stepped inside, the air changed.

Demola greeted them, then excused himself leaving me with a reassuring smile.

Mum's smile froze mid-sentence.

Her eyes flicked to me, narrowing, then she looked away quickly, as though she could erase what she had just seen, but her hand gripped the arm of her chair a little too tightly.

Dad's reaction was slower, more deliberate.

He turned his head, and when his gaze settled on me, his lips parted in shock. His brow furrowed, confusion clouding his face as he stared at me in horror, I almost smiled at his expression.

I know I looked horrible.

Grandma rose before anyone else could move. Her warm smile dissolved instantly, replaced by sharp worry as she moved across the living room.

"Mide, what happened? Did you get into a fight?" she whispered, her voice trembling as she cupped my face with both hands, tilting my chin up so the light revealed everything I had hoped to hide. Her thumb brushed the swollen skin at the corner of my mouth, as she sucked in a breath. "Who di this to you, my child?"

Dad leaned forward, elbows on his knees, his eyes lingering on every bruise as though memorising them. "Mide? What happened?" His voice was calm, but there was steel under it.

Mum finally spoke, her tone clipped though her eyes betrayed unease. "What happened to your face?" Her gaze swept over me again, sharp and searching, as if the bruises themselves were accusing her of something.

The room fell silent, the weight of their stares pressing down on me. I wanted to disappear, but Granny's hands stayed firm, protective, like she was trying to shield me with her touch.

Aunty Amaka sat down across from my parents. "That's why I am here," she said, her voice steady. "To talk about her injuries."

As soon as the words left her mouth, Mum sprang out of her chair, frustration bubbling over almost instantly.

"What has she done this time?!" she demanded, her voice sharp with irritation.

"What?" Aunty Amaka blinked, clearly surprised by the outburst, but Mum ignored her completely and turned her fury on me.

"Mide! Are you the only child I have? Must it always be you? What have you done this time?" Mum continued shouting, ignoring my father's warning glance.

"Toke, what is it? Did anyone say she did something?" Aunty Amaka's voice remained calm but firm, her gaze steady on Mum. "Sit down. Let's talk."

"Aah. I will sit oh. I will sit." Mum huffed as she sank back into her seat, though not without shaking a finger at me. Her eyes roamed over my bruised face again, her voice cutting. "Ṣe orí iwọ? You see what I've been saying, Mide? Always you, I won't be surprised you got into a fight!"

Her words hurt, how could she blame me when she didn't even know what had occurred, no wonder the first person I ran to was Demola's mum, my own mother would not care if I dropped dead before her, and the realisation hurt.

Granny, who had been watching quietly, finally spoke, her eyes never leaving the injury on my lip. "Toke, let us hear what Amaka has to say. Stop accusing the child before you know the full story."

"Thank you, Mama," Aunty Amaka said, nodding gratefully at her. She then turned to my father, who hadn't moved, but sat quietly, his gaze fixed on me, his expression unreadable.

"There's no easy way to say this," Aunty Amaka began, her voice heavy with the seriousness of the situation. "Mide came to see me this morning, and after examining her, I've placed her on a very strong antibiotic to prevent a chance of her, getting an infection."

The room fell silent at her words.

Mum's eyes widened, her face tightening with shock. "What? An infection? From where?" Her voice was low, but panic was already rising. "How? How on earth will she get one?" Her hands flew to her head as she stood again, her worry spilling into rage. "You see! Shey, you want to be stubborn? I warned you about all the rubbish you eat! I always knew you would bring shame to this family and now look! This is exactly what I feared!"

"Toke, please," Aunty Amaka interjected, keeping her voice as calm as she could.

"Please what? What type of infection do you think, she might get? Aah Mide!" Mum's voice resonated, cutting across the room.

Aunty Amaka leaned forward, steadying herself. "I'm treating Mide with antibiotics to prevent her from getting any STDs, but if you just—" she tried to continue, but Mum cut her off.

"Jesu!" Mum breathed, half-scream, half-prayer. She jumped up and clapped her hands together, face flushing. "How? STD ke? So tan! You see! When I said you would disgrace this family, your father and Mama were supporting you. Now just imagine—"

"Listen!" Aunty Amaka's voice rose, small but commanding. The single word snapped Mum's litany short. "Something bad happened to Mide, and we need to focus on helping her, not blaming her."

Mum froze, her eyes travelling over my face as if searching for an explanation written on my skin. "What do you mean something bad happened?" she asked, quieter now but trembling with disbelief.

Aunty Amaka looked at me as if asking my permission to continue, then said quietly; "Mide was raped on her way home from lesson yesterday evening, she came to see Demola, who brought her to me, as she was worried about the pain she was experiencing when she tried to pee. I placed her on a prophylactic dose of antibiotics immediately as she is a survivor of a sexual assault. From the tests done in the hospital, I can confirm Mide was raped."

Her words hit the air like stones.

I almost laughed out as Mum made a small sound— "Eh?"—and then slumped into the chair behind her, as if the world had cracked open.

Instead, I froze, my body trembling, every nerve alight with pain I could not escape. My lips throbbed, my bruised cheek a dull, relentless ache. My chest felt tight, like it was being squeezed, and each breath was a reminder of everything I couldn't undo. My stomach churned with a mix of fear and shame, and a cold wave of nausea swept over me, tears burned behind my eyes, tears that i wouldn't allow fall. It was as though my body itself had decided to hold the pain inside, making me feel heavier and smaller, trapped within myself.

The room spun, sounds distant, the voices around me hollow echoes.

At last, my father's voice cut through the haze, calm and steady, "Mide, are you alright? Do you need a seat? Do you want to stay here for this conversation, or would you prefer to go to your room?"

I wanted to run, to escape the weight pressing down from every direction, but my legs felt like lead. The pain in my body mirrored the ache in my chest, sharp, unrelenting, impossible to ignore but my dad's voice was soft, an offered hand through the storm and I took it.

I nodded, grateful for the chance to escape.

He gave a small, approving incline of his head and so I turned and hurried upstairs, desperate for the thin refuge of my bedroom door. Once inside, I closed the door and leaned against it, breathing shallow and trying to steady my pulse.

The silence of my room felt fragile and safe; but muffled voices floated up from below, proof that nothing could be shut away. Mum's voice grew louder; her anger returned like a tide. "This is your fault!" she shouted. "I told you it wasn't safe! Letting her go to lessons by herself, walking alone, it's all because of you, you caused this to happen!"

Downstairs, Dad said little. He listened and absorbed everything; his silence was not a sign of agreement, but a quiet, steady presence that refused to fuel her rage.

By the time I crept downstairs, Granny had already gone up to her room.

Mum's voice still echoed through the house, sharp fragments of accusation, fear, and frustration ricocheting off the walls. I lingered at the top of the stairs, guilt pressing against my chest, though I knew none of this was my fault. I folded myself small on the stairs, curling in on my bruised, aching body, and watched the people who were supposed to protect me argue over my life as if it were theirs to judge.

All I wanted was to be seen, not as the shame, not as the mistakes, not as the scandal but simply as the child they loved. I wanted someone to look at me and remember me as I was, before the world had hurt me, before the assault had stolen my sense of safety.

Chapter Nine

It wasn't easy to begin healing from what I had gone through, but I was grateful for the support of my dad, Granny, Demola, and aunty Amaka. Their presence and constant reassurances made the weight a little lighter.

It gave me the assurance that the world was a little safer, was it really?

I was grateful for the support shown me, from all of them, all of them, except my Mum. She froze me out, avoided me as though I was the plague. It was my Mum who had been against my dad going to the police, ashamed of what people might say.

Ashamed that the world would see me as the girl who had been raped.

Deep down, I knew she blamed me. She never said it outright, but it was there in every rebuke, in every complaint about the "skimpy" outfits I wore, and in every evening, I stayed out late. Her disapproval wrapped around me like a constant shadow, reminding me that even within my own family, I was not entirely safe from judgment.

Demola, though, was my anchor.

He stayed true to his word, going to school from home just so he could be around me and every day, without fail, he brought me snacks from Mr. Biggs, chocolates and little treats to make me smile. His effort wasn't lost on me; his presence wasn't something I just appreciated; I needed it. He made me feel safe in a way no one else did.

One evening, he brought me one of my favourite snacks, meat pie from Mr. Biggs and a chilled bottle of Fanta. I laughed when he handed it over.

"You always know how to bribe me," I teased, trying to keep things light.

"I do what I can," he said with a wink, settling beside me on the couch. "Plus, I can't have you looking sad all the time."

"Thanks, Demo," I said, but my voice was quieter than I intended.

He didn't miss it.

"Hey," he said, turning slightly to face me, his expression soft. "You know I'm here for you, right?"

I nodded, my throat tightening. "I know." If only he knew I was starting to dream of him in ways, I shouldn't have been doing.

He reached over and gave my hand a gentle squeeze. "Good."

As much as I tried to hide it, I couldn't stop the daydreams.

What if Demola and I could be more than friends? I found myself imagining a future where we lived together, where the safety I felt with him was permanent. It was a silly fantasy, but it was one that brought me comfort in the darkest moments.

I looked forward to his visits each day but was frustrated that he only treated me as a sister.

Then one day, everything changed.

I was walking to a supermarket in the estate when I saw Demola's car driving through the estate gate. He was chatting to a lady in the passenger seat, a very beautiful light skinned lady with long braids and skin so beautiful, she glowed.

They seemed so comfortable together, and it hit me like a punch to the gut.

I was jealous. The realisation caught me completely off guard. I hadn't realized just how much I cared until I saw them both chatting and smiling at each other as though they had only eyes for each other.

Pretending not to notice them, I walked past, but Demola spotted me.

"Hey, Mide! Come say hi."

I ignored him and kept walking.

My heart raced, and a lump formed in my throat. What had I been thinking? That Demola, with his good looks, charm, and everything, would choose someone like me? Someone who was still trying to piece herself together, still carrying so much pain. Someone still in secondary school? Ha ha...it was truly laughable.

He honked a few times, but I pretended not to see him.

He called out to me. I chose to ignore him, and it hurt. As I watched the car drive off, I felt a sting of regret. But that was short-lived because, a few minutes later, I heard footsteps behind me. I felt tense as I turned around, releasing my breath when I saw Demola running toward me, slightly out of breath.

"Hey!" he called as he got closer.

I ignored him and continued walking, but he gently grabbed my arm to stop me. "Wait up!"

"Why?!" I snapped and shoved his hand away.

I didn't stop walking. I didn't even turn to look at him. "What do you want, Demola?" I asked, trying to keep my voice steady, though I could feel the emotions bubbling beneath the surface.

He grabbed my arm gently, pulling me to a stop. "What's up with you?" he asked, his brows furrowed in confusion.

I shrugged, keeping my expression neutral. "The sky is what's up." I said again. "Let me go."

He chuckled, clearly amused by my attempt to deflect, but I wasn't in the mood for jokes. "Are you ignoring me?" he asked, still smiling as if he couldn't understand what was going on.

"What do you want?" I asked again, my voice sharper than I intended.

smile faded a little, and his eyes widened in surprise.

"You. I want you." I wondered if he had been sent to ruin me because I couldn't describe how his words made me feel.

"Me how?"

"I called out to you, you ignored me," he said, his voice gentler now, like he was trying to understand what he'd done wrong.

"Why are you calling me? Don't you have a friend in your car?" I said casually then I realised I just confessed to seeing him.

"Aah, so you were ignoring me?" he said smiling.

"May be." I shrugged.

"Why? What did I do wrong?

I crossed my arms, feeling the frustration build inside me. "Why do you want to know? You looked busy with your girlfriend just now." I snapped.

He blinked, confused at first, then the realisation seemed to dawn on him. A slow smile crept onto his face. "Wait... are you jealous?"

"Haa! Me? Jealous of who?" I retorted, my face heating up. I was caught, and I hated it. I crossed my arms tighter, trying to put some emotional distance between us.

He chuckled, still clearly amused. "I just offered her a lift from the gate. That's it, she just moved into the house opposite mine." he explained, shaking his head, the smile never leaving his face.

"I don't care," I muttered, brushing past him again. But before I could get far, he caught me—this time wrapping an arm around my shoulders. It was casual. Like he would normally do to me and Labisi, but the warmth of his body next to mine confused me. It made it hard to stay mad. Since my attack, I never let anybody close to me again.

Demola was the only person whose touch I welcomed. It felt odd because I couldn't explain why.

"Stop it now. Okay, I'm sorry," he whispered in my ear, his voice was low and teasing. I could hear the smile in his words.

I sighed, feeling my resolve weaken but not ready to give in just yet. I wished I was older, someone who could brush off moments like this without feeling so out of place. "Okay, next time," he continued, "I'll drop my passenger before I call out to you."

"Mtscheew," I hissed, but even that didn't come out with much force. I tried to shake him off, but a part of me didn't want him to let go. Why did he have to make me feel this way?

Did he even know what he was doing to me?

Demola laughed lightly. "Na wa oh. One would think you were my wife with the way you're acting."

"Mtscheew," I hissed again, but there was no real annoyance left in me. His teasing was making it harder to stay mad.

He finally loosened his hold on me but turned me to face him with a rather serious expression. "Mide wait. I don't like seeing you upset. I'm sorry... really."

I looked up at him, feeling the tension in me deflate. "I believe you," I said, unable to stop the small smile tugging at my lips. "I'm just tired." I added, which was a lie.

"Good," he replied, his own smile returning. "Let's walk together."

"Okay." I said smiling as he fell into step beside me.

When we reached my house, I turned to him, wanting to thank him properly but he was staring at me. It was a bit intense. As if he was seeing something magnificent for the first time.

"Thanks, Demo...for everything." I said, shakingly. "You know I go back to school tomorrow, right?"

He nodded before, he caught my arm again and pulled me into a hug.

It wasn't like the casual hugs we'd shared before—this one felt... different. I froze for a second, glancing around to make sure no one was watching, but then I relaxed, sinking into the embrace.

He pulled back slightly and looked down at me. "Don't ever tell me to let you go," he whispered, and before I could respond, he kissed my forehead, then kissed me lightly on the cheek—brief, tender kisses that left me speechless.

Then, without another word, he pushed me gently toward the gate and turned to leave. Normally, he would wait until I went inside before leaving, but tonight, he seemed in a hurry, almost like he needed to get away.

I stood there, watching him go, my hand pressed to my forehead and my cheeks, where his lips had touched. The kiss was like a mark I didn't want to wash away. And truth be told, when I had a shower that evening, I didn't wash my face. I couldn't stop smiling, my mind spinning from the brief but powerful moment we had just shared.

Maybe Demola was never going to see me as a potential girlfriend candidate, but he was protective of me, he cared about me.

And that was enough to keep me satisfied.

Chapter Ten

I couldn't believe, I was on my way out of secondary school.

It felt surreal, knowing that we were all about to go our separate ways, off to different universities, to start new chapters in our lives.

The last day of exams was the craziest we ever had. It was fun watching the excitement. However, I didn't engage much. I did the little I could, but that was it.

As I sat in the hall, waiting for my name to be called, I felt a sense of pride knowing I had done my best and it was good enough. My dad had already planned my next steps, of course. He was always a step ahead, making sure I had everything I needed for the future. He wanted me to attend a computer school before heading to university, as he thought it would give me an edge. I didn't mind, though. I liked the idea of being prepared, of feeling like I was entering the next stage of life with confidence.

There seemed to be good news all around. Alaba had just passed her junior WAEC, and she was glowing with pride, already talking about what it would be like to move on to senior secondary school. Taiye, our academic star, had received a full scholarship to pursue her PhD in UCLA.

Our parents were beyond thrilled.

"So, what's the plan?" Isioma asked, her voice full of excitement as we finally walked out of the school hall, clutching our little trophies. The energy from the prize-giving ceremony was still high, and we were practically glowing. Between Isioma, Halima and I, we had taken home nine awards out of the twenty-three awards presented.

Halima, ever graceful, had snagged an appreciation award for her role as head girl, and of course, she had also won the best-dressed award—no surprise there.

Isioma, always competitive, had won the science award, along with awards for music and accounting. I went home with awards for maths, further maths, and economics.

"Are you still going to the end-of-year party?" Isioma asked again, her eyes gleaming with mischief as she adjusted her schoolbag.

Halima chimed in before I could answer, "Which one? If you mean the Rotimi's party, count me out. You know my mum doesn't like them. I don't like them either."

Isioma rolled her eyes dramatically. "That's the one. Bimpe invited all the 'who's who' at school. I still can't believe I got an invite. I'm counting myself lucky she even noticed me!"

I raised an eyebrow at that. "You or me? We have never even spoken, so I am surprised I got an invite from her too."

It was true.

Bimpe and I had been in the same school since JSS1, which was the start of junior secondary, but in all those years, we had never exchanged more than a polite nod in passing.

Now, out of nowhere, she was acting like we were old friends.

"Mide, it's your 'fine girl' status she likes," Isioma teased, nudging me playfully. "Who wouldn't want to have a fine friend?"

I laughed, shaking my head. "Isioma, are you saying you are my friend because I am fine?"

"Of course! It's a bonus to be seen with a fine girl na," Isioma said with a wide grin.

I pretended to be annoyed but couldn't hide my smile. "You're not serious, Isioma. Naughty girl."

"But seriously," Isioma said, her tone turning playful, "You are a fine girl oh, and you changed in the last few years! Hmm!"

"I know." Halima nodded in agreement.

I could feel my cheeks heating up. "Isi, it's enough oh." I mumbled, trying to change the subject. But Isioma wasn't the type to let something like that go.

"Aah, it's not enough!" she exclaimed, clearly enjoying herself. She gestured with her hands, outlining my figure in an exaggerated way. "Look at those hips now, and that... figure!"

"You're crazy," I said to her, already walking ahead to escape the teasing.

"If I didn't know better, I would think you've been eating the forbidden fruit," Isioma said, her voice loud enough to turn a few heads.

"Isioma!" Halima gasped, half-shocked and half-amused. "Gaskiya, this your mouth will put you in trouble one day."

Halima, ever the composed one, had become the voice of reason among the three of us. She used to be the quiet one, but now, she was the glue that held our dynamic trio together, balancing out Isioma's playful chaos.

"Don't mind her," I said, waving off Isioma's words as I tried to suppress my laughter. "Her mouth is too sharp."

Isioma grinned. "You know you love me."

"I'm going home. Let me know if we're going to the party," I said, brushing past the teasing.

Halima tilted her head slightly, her eyes studying me. "Are you actually considering going, Mide?"

"Not really," I admitted. "My mind isn't on it."

"Then follow your mind," Halima said, matter-of-factly. "Bimpe is not your friend anyway."

"Abi?" I sighed, feeling a bit conflicted. "But wouldn't it be rude to ignore her invitation? I mean, it's her first time inviting me to something."

"How would it be rude?" Halima asked, raising an eyebrow. "She's never invited you to anything before, so why worry now?"

"I just feel like... I don't know, it's her first time extending an invite, and I don't want to seem like I'm snubbing her."

Halima looked thoughtful for a moment before shaking her head. "My dear, you don't owe her anything. If you don't want to go, don't go. Simple."

Isioma, who had been unusually quiet during this exchange, suddenly piped up. "Misery loves company! Halima just doesn't want you to go because she's not going," she teased, nudging Halima playfully.

Halima rolled her eyes at Isioma's antics, but she couldn't help smiling. "Mide, don't listen to her. Follow your mind."

I laughed at their playful banter, feeling a bit lighter as I walked home with them. Isioma and Halima continued their back-and-forth as we walked, throwing playful jabs at each other. Their laughter filled the air reminding me of why I cherished our friendship so much.

They knew how to lift my spirits, no matter the situation.

Finally, I turned to them and smiled. "Let's see," I said. "I'll let you know what I decide."

Isioma and Halima exchanged a glance, their teasing temporarily paused. "Whatever you choose girl, we've got your back," Isioma said with a wink.

Halima nodded in agreement. "Exactly. Even if it means you attending."

I smiled.

*** * * ***

I decided to attend Bimpe's party with Isioma.

Halima was adamant about not attending and made it clear she didn't approve but wasn't going to stop us from attending the party.

"I want to hear everything when you get back." she said before blowing a kiss and ending the call.

I took my time getting dressed that day. It was nothing flamboyant. Just a pair of blue jeans and a grey body-hugging top that fit me perfectly, with a pair of black loafers Taiye had sent to me from America. She was always trying to keep us up to date with the latest fashion there. I tied my kinky hair into a neat bun. Back then, it was just wash, plait, and let it grow—no complicated routines, yet it always managed to thrive, thick and full like grass. Hair care used to be so simple.

Isioma arrived early, as expected. Her presence always seemed to electrify the air. She walked in confidently, wearing a beautiful red bandage dress. The type we call body con now. Her hair was newly permed and slicked back with a sleek band, making her look effortlessly chic. I did ask her once why she loved the colour red. She simply answered that she was an Igbo girl.

With her fair skin, the red did wonders for her complexion.

"You look hot!" she said, her eyes scanning me approvingly as soon as I opened the door.

"Oh girl!" I laughed, admiring her bold outfit. "You look good too!" I shook my head. "I love your outfit, Isioma; I could never pull off something like that."

Isioma spun playfully in her dress; her energy was infectious. "Thank you, thank you! So, are we ready?"

"Yeah," I replied, grabbing my waist bag and wristwatch. "Halima isn't coming, right?"

Isioma sighed dramatically, crossing her arms. "No, her mum really doesn't like the Rotimi's. I respect her for standing by her decision."

I teased her with a playful nudge. "Hmm, should we also skip this party then?"

She rolled her eyes and gave me a light shove. "You wish! We're going. Let's not get too responsible now."

I chuckled, adjusting my bag.

"I can't believe your Mum let you attend this party," Isioma said.

Even I was surprised at how relaxed Mum had been about the party. Normally, she would have interrogated me with a million questions about where I was going and with whom, but today, she had simply told me to come back early and be careful. Granny was sitting on the balcony as we left the house, she waved at us, not forgetting to admire us and remind us of how beautiful we were.

We had only gone a few blocks when I spotted Aunty Amaka's car approaching. She was seated in the passenger seat, looking regal as always. They slowed down when they were close then I noticed, it wasn't her driver but Demola who was driving his mother.

"Chai!" I whispered under my breath.

"What's up?" Isioma asked.

"Nothing." I quickly said. "I forgot my lip gloss at home, but it's alright. Let's go."

"Omalicha! Beautiful girls! Where are you off to?" Aunty Amaka called out as the car slowed down beside us.

"Good afternoon, Dr. Adetokunbo," Isioma greeted, her voice full of respect.

"Good afternoon, Aunty," I added with a smile. "We're off to a friend's end-of-year party."

"Good afternoon, Demo." I added, smiling at him.

Isioma gave Demola a polite nod. "Good afternoon," she said.

Demola remained silent, lost in thought as he stared at me. His mother, noticing the awkwardness, nudged him lightly on the arm. "Demola, they're speaking to you," she said, her eyes twinkling with a knowing smile.

He blinked, snapping out of whatever thoughts had been running through his head. "Oh, err... Hi," he mumbled, clearly caught off guard and a little embarrassed which caused his mother to smile.

I stifled a laugh, glancing at Isioma. She raised an eyebrow at me, her look saying, well, that was awkward.

Aunty Amaka smiled warmly. "Alright dears. Let us not keep you. Enjoy your party. Hmm... Mide," she added, her tone teasing, "you're becoming a real swan oh. These boys of mine should start looking for wives among you and your friends."

My cheeks flamed with embarrassment, and I could see that Isioma was equally flustered. We quickly mumbled our goodbyes and hurried down the road, eager to escape the situation.

Chapter eleven

The party was already in full swing by the time we arrived. The music was so loud it thumped from the speakers, vibrating through the walls and into the ground beneath my feet. The place was packed full of classmates, some familiar faces and others I only knew in passing.

A wave of excitement hit me as we stepped inside.

This was the real deal.

We were older now.

"Hi, beautiful!" Bimpe's high-pitched voice pierced through the music as she spotted us from across the room, making her way toward us with arms wide open and a wide smile, I almost groaned out loud, when Isioma winked at me and disappeared. She noticed how Bimpe totally ignored her presence.

"Hi," I greeted, offering a small, polite smile. I leaned in as she pulled me into a hug, her perfume overwhelming as she kissed the air beside my cheeks.

"Thanks for inviting me."

"No, thank *you* for coming," she replied in her exaggerated, fake American accent that grated on my nerves. "Come, I'll introduce you to my friends," she added, grabbing my hand and pulling me deeper into the house.

I followed her reluctantly, my stomach tightening with unease as I followed her. Something was off. I could feel it in the way Bimpe smiled, in the way her eyes flicked to me and away, as if she was sizing me up. But I reminded myself I was there to have fun. I was there to enjoy myself, not overthink things.

We reached a group of seven or so people, boys and girls lounging on couches, leaning against the walls, all draped over each other in ways that made me feel uncomfortable. They touched each other casually, too casually. With hands lingering on shoulders, arms wrapped around waists, legs intertwined.

I swallowed, feeling suddenly out of place.

"These are my friends from my primary school," Bimpe announced in that accent, sweeping her hand in a dramatic gesture. "And guys, this is Mide," she added, as if introducing someone important, like I was some kind of exhibit.

"Hi, nice to meet you all," I said, forcing another smile, though my discomfort grew by the second.

One of the boys, tall with a piercing in his eyebrow, eyed me up and down. His gaze was heavy, lingering too long on my body. "You're pretty," he said, his voice low and suggestive.

The way he said it, the way he looked at me made my skin crawl. I felt exposed, vulnerable. I needed to get away. "Thanks, I… uh… need to find my friend," I stammered, pointing a finger backward and backing away from the group before they could respond.

As I walked off, snippets of their conversation floated behind me.

"Is that her?" one of the girls asked, her tone dripping with disdain.

"Doesn't seem like much," another girl replied, her voice sharp.

"I agree with Musty," the boy who had complimented me said, and I could hear the smirk in his voice. "She's pretty though."

"Really hot." Mustapha added.

But it was Bimpe's words that cut the deepest.

"…yeah, that's her, and she thinks she's all that. Stuck-up bitch!"

I didn't hear the rest. I didn't need to. My heart sank; a cold lump began forming in my throat. Why was she calling me names? Why had she even invited me if she thought that way of me?

Was this some kind of cruel setup?

I pushed through the crowd. My vision blurred as tears threatened to spill over. The laughter, the music, the energy of the party—none of it reached me. I was lost in a whirlwind of emotions: hurt, anger, betrayal. I needed to leave. I needed to get out of there.

I was so caught up in my thoughts that I didn't see who I bumped into.

I started apologising when he spoke "Sorry." I whispered hurriedly.

"It's fine," Demola said from above.

I looked up, wondering if my day could be any worse and my heart stopped. Of all people to run into, it had to be him. Why now? I couldn't deal with this, with him, not after everything that had just happened. What was he even doing here? I mean it was good to see him but not at that point where I felt I just wanted to be alone and figure out why I was there.

"Are you okay?" he asked, concern written all over his face as his eyes searching mine.

"Yes, leave me alone, please," I snapped pushing past him in a haste to get out of here. I didn't want to talk. I didn't want to explain. I just wanted to disappear. Where was Isioma?

I found Isioma mingling with a group from school, laughing, dancing, carefree as usual. From where I stood, she looked so at ease, so comfortable in her own skin, and I envied her for it. Usually, I was the one who brought the energy, who danced and laughed and made everyone feel at home.

But not anymore.

Since the attack last year, everything had changed. I had changed. I was quieter now, more withdrawn, always looking over my shoulder. Every man I saw, every group of boys, made my heart race with fear. It was like they were all potential threats, lurking in the shadows, waiting to pounce. My sense of humour, my confidence, had been stripped away, leaving behind a shell of who I used to be.

Apart from Kenny, Demola, his mother, my parents, granny, and the people who had hurt me, no one knew what had happened to me. To everyone else, I had simply grown quieter, more reserved.

I stood there, surrounded by people having fun, but feeling utterly disconnected from it all. It was like I was watching the party from the outside, unable to join in, unable to feel what everyone else was feeling.

I didn't belong there.

"Are you going to just stand there or are you going to share a drink with me?" a voice interrupted my thoughts, pulling me from the swirl of emotions and confusion.

"Huh?" I turned around to find Mustapha, Bimpe's smooth-talking friend, standing there with a cup in hand, his smile wide and confident. He had that kind of easy grin that probably made girls swoon without effort, and I could see why. Despite the unsettling tension that had been brewing since I arrived, I forced a polite smile but instinctively stepped back, creating some space between us.

He was the one who had described me as 'hot'.

"It's rude to keep someone's hand hanging," he teased, still holding the cup out towards me.

"Oh, sorry," I mumbled, feeling a little cornered. "But thank you, I'm fine." I tried to keep my tone light, though something kept telling me telling me to leave.

"So, you're rejecting my drink?" His grin didn't waver, but there was a playful challenge behind his words that made my discomfort deepen. He wasn't used to hearing "no," that much was obvious.

Just as I was about to refuse again, loud laughter broke through the crowd. I glanced over to see Demola, standing by Bimpe's brother, Dotun, and a few other people. That was when I remembered.

Demola and Dotun were in university together.

That was why he was here. One of the girls was clinging to Demola as if she was an accessory attached to him. She was laughing at something he'd said. Why did some girls do that by the way? As if they were trying to send a message to others. Well, I got the message and for some reason, it sent a strange wave of jealousy crashing over me. Why did I care? I didn't even understand why it bothered me so much, but seeing him with another girl, clad in shorts open at the waist and a bikini top looking so at ease, stirred something in me I couldn't ignore.

At that exact moment, Demola's eyes locked with mine, and something inside me had me making decisions I shouldn't have. I didn't know why, but I felt a sudden need to prove something to him and to myself. Maybe I just didn't want to feel like I was fading into the background. Without thinking, I flashed

Mustapha my best smile and took the drink he offered, allowing my fingers brush his as I accepted it. I even looped my arm through his when he offered it, it terrified me, but I couldn't stop myself. This was about Demola. I wanted to show him I could have someone's attention too, that I mattered too.

"I'm Mustapha," he said as we started walking towards the pool area, his voice was low and casual.

"Mide," I replied with a forced chuckle, trying to shake off the strange unease bubbling in my chest. "But you already know that."

"Of course I do," he said with a smile that seemed too practiced. "And I also know you heard some of the... uh, not-so-kind things back there." His tone was light, but his eyes flicked towards me, studying my reaction.

"What?" I asked, pretending to be clueless, even though my stomach knotted at the reminder of the girls' harsh whispers.

His laugh was low and knowing. "Come on, you know... those girls were talking about you when you walked away."

"Oh, that." I muttered, suddenly feeling the weight of their judgment pressing down on me again. A wave of discomfort washed over me, making me wish I had just stayed home.

"Yeah, but you know, it's just typical," Mustapha continued, shrugging casually. "Girls hating on each other. I never really get it. What's the point?"

I sighed, trying to brush it off. "You would have to ask them. They are your friends, not mine."

Mustapha chuckled again, clearly enjoying the banter. "Fair enough. You don't talk much, do you?"

"I do...or I used to," I said, my voice coming out sharper than I intended. "But like I tell anyone who asks, I'm older now."

"Older?" he laughed, genuinely surprised. "You're sixteen, right? You're not sixty!"

"Feels like it sometimes," I said under my breath, thinking about how much had changed in just one year. The reminder caused me to gently try freeing my hand.

He smiled, leaning in closer, as if we were sharing a secret. "So, what do I have to do to become your friend?"

"Don't you have enough friends already?" I shot back, half-teasing but also genuinely curious why he was so persistent.

"One can never have too many friends," he replied smoothly, that confident grin never leaving his face.

"Really?" I asked, still unsure why he was so eager to strike up a friendship with me of all people.

"Yes, really," he said, holding up his cup again. "Come on, let's toast to being friends."

I hesitated, my eyes flicking towards the cup in my hand. "I may never see you again."

"You're not dying, are you?" he joked, making me laugh despite myself. "You laugh!" he said in feign disbelief.

"No, I'm not, but still..."

"Cheers to meeting you, Mide," he said, cutting me off as his cup clinked lightly against mine.

"Okay, fine. Cheers to meeting you Mustapha." I said reluctantly, taking a sip of the drink. It tasted strange—sweeter than I expected, but with a bitter aftertaste that made me frown.

"What's this?" I asked, glancing at him.

"Just punch. No alcohol, if that's what you're worried about," he assured me with a wink.

"Are you sure?" I asked, raising an eyebrow as I looked at the glass in my hand.

"Definitely," he said, flashing that same confident smile. "It's made for non-alcoholics like you."

Before I could respond, he leaned in a little closer, his voice dropping to a whisper. "Trust me."

I felt a twinge of unease. When had he gotten so close? He brushed my cheek with his finger, and though I instinctively stepped back, it wasn't far enough to break the tension building between us. There was a strange feeling creeping up on me. I took another sip of the punch, trying to focus on the party all the time stealing a glance at Demola. We chatted for a bit longer, and I even found myself laughing at some of his jokes. But something still felt off, like I wasn't fully in control.

After another cup of punch, Mustapha asked me to dance.

I stood up, but the second I did, the world tilted sharply. I quickly sat back down, pressing my hand against my forehead, trying to steady myself.

"No, please God. Not again." I whispered under my breath. My body suddenly felt frozen with fear.

"Are you okay?" Mustapha asked, his voice filled with concern as he leaned down to check on me.

I didn't get the chance to respond.

"What's wrong?" Demola's voice cut through the noise like a sharp blade, and I blinked slowly, trying to focus. He walked over to us and knelt beside me gently. "Mide?"

"Hmmm... what do you want?" I slurred, my voice sounding distant and strange to my own ears.

"Are you drunk?" Demola asked, his tone hardening as he turned to Mustapha. "What did you give her?"

"Nothing!" Mustapha said quickly, raising his hands in defence. There was genuine surprise in his voice.

"Nothing?" Demola sneered.

"She just had some punch." Mustapha answered. He sounded frightened.

"Punch?" Demola repeated, his disbelief evident. He glanced over at Bimpe's brother, Dotun, who was still standing nearby with his guests. "Dotun!"

"Stop shouting." I said holding my head. A request Demola seemed to ignore as he called out to his friend a second time.

Dotun jogged over, looking confused as he glanced between us. "What's up?"

"What's in this drink?" Demola demanded, holding up the cup.

Dotun shrugged casually. "I don't understand."

"What's in the punch." Demola demanded. He sounded angry.

"Oh." Dotun said. "Regular lacing, guy. Nothing big."

"Nothing big?" Demola's voice was tight with anger. "These are high school students Dotun. I wouldn't touch that stuff. Why would you serve it here?"

"Guy, calm down now," Dotun said, trying to diffuse the situation. "Is she your girl?"

That comment earned him a withering glare from Demola, wiping the teasing smile right off Dotun's face. "Sorry, man," he muttered. "Look, she can chill in one of the rooms—"

"No," Demola cut him off, his voice firm. "I'll take her home."

Turning back to me, Demola softened his tone. The switch was one I couldn't comprehend. His hand gently resting on my shoulder. "Can you walk?"

"I don't need your help. Mustapha let's dance." I mumbled, even though the room continued to spin wildly around me. I felt if I could just sit for a while, I'd feel better in no time. I knew what was happening around me. It was the strength to do as I wished that I didn't have.

"Yes, you do," Demola said, ignoring my request.

"Mustapha." I called out gently.

"He's gone." Came Demola's swift reply. "And yes, I chased him away."

"You bully." I said as I hit his shoulder before I passed out.

Chapter Twelve

I came to as Demola carefully helped me into the passenger seat of his car, making sure I was sitting upright before handing me a bottle of water.

"Drink this," he said gently, as he scanned my face.

I took a sip. The cool water was a soothing welcome to the dryness in my throat. Demola wet a handkerchief with some of the water and began wiping my face. His touch was so calming and careful, as if he thought that I might break.

"Do you feel better now?" Demola as I blinked a few times, the heaviness in my head slowly fading. The spinning had stopped, but a dull disorientation was still present. As my vision cleared, I realized we were still sitting in his car, the soft glow of streetlights filtering through the windows.

"I feel… better," I mumbled, though my words didn't match the uncertainty swimming in my mind. I rubbed my eyes and glanced around, confused. "Why are we still in your car?"

Demola raised an eyebrow, clearly surprised and wondering if I didn't remember. "Because I couldn't take you home in the state you were in," he explained, his eyes fixed on my face, watching me carefully like he was still unsure if I was okay. "Now, will you answer my question?"

"What question?" I asked, blinking again, trying to recall what he had asked me earlier.

He sighed slowly, a mix of amusement and exasperation in his tone. "I asked if you're better now."

"Oh." I let out a small breath, embarrassed. "Yes, I am," I said, straightening up in my seat.

"Was it the punch? I asked suddenly.

"Yeah." Was his response. I chose not to say anymore on the matter.

"Can I go home then?" suddenly remembering a lot of what I said. I turned red embarrassed.

"Not before I give you a scolding," he said, glancing out the window as if trying to gauge something. "What's your friend's name? I should get her too."

I frowned, the mention of friends stirring unwanted memories of Bimpe and her group—the whispers, the insults. My stomach tightened as I thought back to their words, the fake smiles, and the judgment hidden behind every glance. "I have no friend here," I muttered bitterly, the anger bubbling back up, stronger this time. I hadn't expected to feel so hurt by people I barely knew.

Demola's brow furrowed as he studied me. "The one I saw you with earlier?" He looked like he didn't believe me, like he wasn't ready to let it go. "What about her?"

"Oh, you mean Isioma," I said, snapping out of my thoughts for a moment. "What about her?"

"Do you want us to leave her here?" he asked, his tone teasing but still laced with a hint of responsibility. That was Demola. Never wanting to abandon anyone.

"No, no," I replied quickly. "She's inside somewhere. I just hope she's ready to leave."

He sighed, shaking his head slightly like the responsible older brother figure he always seemed to be. "Just wait here. I'll go and get her. But before I get her, you need to hear this, you don't take drinks from people at a party especially if it's in a cup, you have no idea what they put in drinks like that"

When I said nothing, he rolled his eyes and said, "Mide, anything could have happened to you in there, you don't do that okay, do you understand?"

I nodded and watched as he slipped out of the car and headed back toward the house and disappeared into the crowd, then leaned back into the seat, letting out a deep breath. Everything felt so jumbled in my mind—Mustapha, the strange punch, the jealousy that flared up when I saw Demola with that girl clinging to his arm.

That was the only reason I took that punch.

I closed my eyes, willing my racing thoughts to slow down. It wasn't like me to react this way. Jealousy? Over Demola? It seemed ridiculous, but the emotions were there, whether I wanted them to be or not. And Mustapha, something about that whole encounter had left me feeling uneasy, more so than I wanted to admit.

Maybe he was innocent in all of this. I didn't know. I just wanted to go home. Slowly, I closed my eyes.

A few minutes later, I heard the car door open, and Demola slid back into the driver's seat. "Isioma wants to stay," he said. "She's having a good time, so I didn't tell her about what happened. I figured that it wasn't my story to tell."

I looked at him, feeling an unexpected wave of relief. "Thank you for not telling her." The last thing I wanted was for Isioma to know how vulnerable I had been tonight, or worse, for her to worry.

Demola gave a small nod, his eyes narrowed slightly as they met mine. "You don't have to thank me, Mide," he said gently. "I just want to make sure you're okay."

There was something about the way he said it, something that made me feel seen in a way I hadn't felt in a long time. He cared, deeply, and that realization made me feel safe, even amid all the chaos swirling around in my mind.

"Do you want to go home now?" he asked, his tone gentle but clear, as if giving me the choice to decide what I needed.

I nodded slowly. "Yes, please. I just… I just want to go home."

Without another word, Demola started the car and pulled away from the house.

We drove in silence, and I closed my eyes, letting the rhythm of the car's movement soothe me.

Tonight, had been overwhelming, I wasn't going to lie.

"Thank you," I whispered, not sure if he heard me, but meaning every word. Bottom of Form

Demola slowed the car down and parked just past my house, his fingers curling around the steering wheel as he turned to face me. There was something in his eyes that told me something was brewing.

"I'm going to London in September." he said. If his words were meant to be received with excitement, it didn't happen. They weighed me down instead.

I sat up a little straighter as the meaning of it all sank in. Why was he telling me this now? Anyway, he never stayed long when he travelled so I guess it was okay but there was a finality in his tone that made me uneasy.

"What's going on? Do you have to?" I asked, trying to mask the growing panic inside me.

"Yeah, I do," he replied gently with a smile, but it wasn't unkind.

"How long will you be gone?" My voice came out steadier than I felt, though my heart was already pounding.

"Just over a year, two years or more, who knows" he said with a sigh.

"I sat up fully alarmed. "That's a long time, Demo."

"I know," he said, his tone serious but resigned. "There's a course I want to take, and after that, I'll continue with my master's."

His words hung between us, heavy and suffocating. So, I was going to spend a few years again not seeing Demola? Sometimes I envied the Adetokunbo kids. They travelled to the UK like it was just behind their house. The thought of not seeing him for so long hit me hard. Demola had been a constant presence in my life, always there, always supportive. I felt like someone was pulling a safety net out from under me and this time, it wasn't under my control. It wasn't like when I avoided him for almost two years but still manage to catch glimpse of him from time to time.

This was different.

"I'll miss you," I whispered, barely able to say it out loud.

It was an admission that felt too vulnerable.

"Are you sure?" he teased lightly, his voice softening as he tried to ease the tension between us. "Because a few seconds ago, you couldn't stand me."

Despite myself, I smiled. "I will miss you," I repeated, this time with more conviction.

He chuckled; the sound was so warm. Then, with his right hand, he reached out and ruffled my afro bun. "You've got a lot of hair, Mide. It's beautiful."

"Thank you," I said, my voice almost a whisper as his hand slid from my hair to the back of my neck and his thumb brushed lightly against my skin. For a moment, neither of us moved. His gaze held mine, as if he was searching for something in my eyes, waiting for me to say something, to acknowledge the pull between us. It was a tension that seemed to grow stronger every time we were together, but I couldn't find the words to explain it.

Did he feel it too?

"I have to go in now," I whispered, suddenly feeling overwhelmed by the intensity of the moment.

Demola's hand slipped away from my neck, his eyes still holding that intensity. "Gosh, you've grown, Mide," he said shaking his head, almost like he was talking to himself. "When did that happen?"

"I don't understand," I said, confused by the sudden shift in conversation. "Of course, I've grown. Haven't you grown too?"

He chuckled shaking his head again. "No, you clearly don't understand," he said, his voice low and almost wistful. He slowly reached for the car's ignition. "I'll see you later then."

I thanked him and got out of the car, but as I walked toward my house, the heaviness in my chest didn't lift. There was something more than just the friendship Demola and I shared, more than the brother-sister bond we had always claimed. But how could I put it into words? I didn't know if he felt it too, or if my position in his life as younger sibling was cast in stone.

I only knew it was something and I didn't want to lose it.

September crept up faster than I expected. Between computer school, and the general chaos of family life, I hadn't had much time to visit Demola. Still, the thought of him leaving drummed at the back of my mind like a sort of punishment. I avoided the mini farewell party his family threw for him. I didn't trust myself not to cry in front of him, and the last thing I wanted was for him to see me like that.

I was in love with Demola.

It was true I was just a teenager, and some people would think I wouldn't understand love, but they would be wrong because I knew what love was. Love was what I felt for Demola. That love had been built over the years. There were times I wanted to ask him if he felt what I felt when we were together. I know

Demola loved me, but I wanted a different type of love, not the brotherly one he gave to me.

That was the reason I didn't attend the party.

I was hurting too much.

* * *

The evening, after his farewell party, Demola and his mother walked my mum and Alaba back home. I pretended to be asleep when they came in because I wasn't ready to face him yet, not with the finality of goodbye hanging in the air.

"Mide is resting," I heard my mum say in a low tone after checking on me. "She still isn't feeling too well."

"Rest is good. That child has been reading a lot lately." Aunty Amaka replied, but I heard Demola's voice next, more insistent.

"I'd like to say goodbye. Can I see her?" he said.

What do you think happened next?

No surprise there, my mum allowed him to come into my room. The betrayal. Couldn't she just respect my privacy for once? Now, it wasn't strange that she let him into my room. We were close like that, but as a blooming young lady, you would think she would decline. I felt a wave of panic rise in my chest as I heard his quiet footsteps approach. He knocked gently before stepping inside. The room was dim, but I could see him clearly as he walked toward me as quiet as a mouse.

He sat down on the edge of my bed and watched me.

His touch was soft, hesitant almost, as he brushed the back of his finger against my cheek. The gesture sent a shiver through me, like butterflies fluttering inside my chest.

"Hey…" he whispered in a voice low and filled with emotion. "Mide, am I wrong to think you're avoiding me?"

My heart raced, but I kept my eyes closed, too afraid to face him.

"I don't know why you don't want to see me," he continued, his voice cracking slightly. "And I can't force you." He let out a deep sigh, the sadness in his tone was unmistakable. "I leave early tomorrow morning. You know that, right?"

I lay still, barely breathing, my heart aching.

"I gave Alaba my email," he said gently. "So, you can reach me whenever you want. Just… just let me know if you need anything."

He paused. I could still feel his eyes on me. "But Mide listen, no partying while I'm gone, okay?" He tried to add a touch of humour to his voice, but it didn't ease the tension. "I won't be around to protect you, and no walking alone at night either."

I felt the corners of my lips twitch at his teasing tone, but it did nothing to ease the ache in my chest.

"Meanwhile, your dad says you might be going to a private university. That's amazing." he said. "You're brilliant, my love. You'll do so well."

My breath caught at the words 'my love'.

He sighed again, a softer sound this time. "Just… make sure you tell me everything, okay? Everything that happens at school. I want to hear it all so we can laugh together, okay?"

His voice was so tender and sincere, that it made the ache worse. I wanted to say something, to tell him how much he meant to me, how much I would miss him, but the words stayed stuck in my throat.

"I'm going to go now," he whispered, leaning down to press a soft kiss against my cheek. It wasn't brief. He took his time, then he stood up and left the room, closing the door quietly behind him. As soon as he was gone, I sat up, my heart racing. That was it. He was leaving. I wouldn't see him for who knows how long—a year, maybe more. The thought of it made my chest tighten painfully.

I scrambled out of bed and rushed to the window, just in time to see him and his mum walking through the gate. Demola paused for a moment, turning his head towards my window as if he knew I was watching. I quickly ducked behind the curtain, my heart pounding, hoping he didn't see me.

When I peeked out again, I saw his mum had also stopped. She touched his arm gently, and he turned to her, giving her one of his warm smiles. The kind that made my stomach twist with guilt. Aunty Amaka had this superpower of speaking to her children telepathically. She said something to him, and he nodded before they both continued their journey home. I stood there at the window, feeling the lump in my throat grow heavier. There was a look that had passed between them, one that made me feel guilty for not saying goodbye properly.

And for the first time in weeks, I cried because, as I realised just how much I was going to miss him.

Chapter Thirteen

June 2001

"Aunty Amaka, just left, she brought some gifts for us from Labisi and Demola, I put yours in your room." Alaba told me as soon as I walked into the house.

"Ah, it would have been nice to see Aunty Amaka, since Labisi and her brothers moved to London, we hardly see her again as she was hardly ever around."
I joked as I headed towards my room

"True, she looked amazing, and she says to tell you, you must visit before she goes back to London." Alaba said.

"I will." I threw over my shoulder as I pushed open the door to my room. The first thing I saw was a big Selfridges bag on my bed, excited I dropped my handbag on the floor and rushed to open the bag of goodies Aunty Amaka had dropped off for me. Hmm, Demola and Labisi must have spent some good money on these gifts. As much as I was happy with them, it was the envelope at the bottom of the bag I needed to open desperately. I could feel there was something else in it besides a paper, so I opened it gently.

I was right.

In it was a beautiful chain with a locket, fascinated I raised it up, before I placed it on my bed and pulled out the letter in the envelope. My heart pounded as I sat on my bed and read the letter which I knew had been written by Demola.

Hey Mide,

I hope Mummy does not misplace this letter. How have you been, your family and all? Sorry I didn't make it back at the time I said I would. When I finished my program, I got a job with an IT company which offers a great opportunity. The package is way more than I think I deserve for someone with hardly any job experience really. It's not like I'm underrating myself, but I wasn't expecting it. Anyway, enough about me.

How have you been, school and all? Am I repeating myself? Labisi showed me photos Alaba sent to her. You both have grown so much especially you Mide. Gosh! You've grown into a beautiful young lady.

I hope I can be back within the next few months. Mide I've missed you all. I miss our little quarrels. You know my mum says she envies our relationship because we get on so well. I guess she was right. Wait, how old are you again? Sometimes I think we are mates. My favourite person, I hope you haven't replaced me though. Lol. Anyway, I'm glad Labisi showed me photos. It would be nice to hear from you directly one of these days. I have a question though. It's been a while, but I feel I should ask. Why didn't you want to say goodbye that night? I knew you weren't sleeping. It would have been nice if you had.

I'm rambling, aren't I? I'm just glad I could write to you. I hope all we got for you fit. I hope you get a lovely photo of me to put in that locket (joking). This is my number. I hear we have mobile network in Nigeria now. Great stuff. Do you have a phone? If not, I could send you one. This is my number +44xxxxxxxx/8. Let me know how I can reach you.

**My love always,
Demola.**

As I finished reading the letter, I sat there, completely still. My heart raced as I reread certain lines"" *It would have been nice if you had said goodbye."* and *"I knew you weren't sleeping?"*

So, he had noticed.

I held the letter in one hand and touched the locket with the other. It was beautiful—white gold, glimmering softly under the light. The fact that he had thought to include something so personal, something that would rest close to my heart, made me feel warm inside. He joked about me putting his photo inside, but now, as I touched the locket, my only thought was doing exactly that.

I stood up and walked to the mirror and put the chain on. My fingers traced the delicate chain around my neck, and I couldn't help but smile. Demola had always been more than a friend, and the way he spoke to me in the letter made it clear he felt something too, even if he didn't come right out and say it. He was giving me space, time to grow and letting me figure things out, but still letting me know he cared deeply.

I sat back down on the bed, staring at the letter, rereading the parts where he mentioned missing me, the photos, and the fact that he didn't want me to replace him as my best friend.

How could I replace you, Demo? I thought to myself.

The truth was no one else could take his place. No one else understood me the way he did, and no one else made me feel the way he did.

With Demola, I felt safe, protected, cherished.

* * *

October, came and I headed to Uni.

Stepping onto the university campus felt like entering a whole new world. The thrill of being called a university student quickly faded when I realized how hard it was to make new friends. I found myself keeping my distance, as old trust issues from the past still followed me like a shadow and the attention from the opposite sex only made me feel more out of place.

Instead of making new friends, I threw myself into my studies. It was easier to lose myself in books and assignments than deal with the uneasiness that crept in whenever I was around unfamiliar faces, especially men.

Halima had settled well into her life in Chicago, and Isioma was miles away in Nsukka, Eastern Nigeria. We kept in touch through long phone calls, thanks to mobile network, but it wasn't the same. I missed them, their laughter, and the comfort of knowing they were by my side. Christmas was just around the corner, and I couldn't wait to see Isioma who was coming to Lagos.

After the disastrous party at Bimpe's, I had finally told her everything that had happened—well, almost everything. I conveniently left out the part about Demola, still not ready to unpack whatever was brewing there.

Isioma, as expected, didn't hold back.

"That girl is a witch! I swear!" Isioma fumed, her hands gesturing wildly as she paced back and forth.

Her face was a mix of disbelief and anger.

I couldn't help but laugh. "She's just nasty. You should've heard how her friends talked about me that night."

"If I had been there, I would've gone back in and given it back to her!" Isioma spat, still heated. "You know me—I don't have time for rubbish."

"I know, Isi," I said, shaking my head. "That's exactly why I kept my mouth shut. I didn't want you turning the party upside down."

Isioma gave me a side-eye. "You're lucky you didn't tell Halima either. That one would've given us a lecture."

I burst out laughing. "Halima told us not to go! We would never hear the end of it."

"Omo, Bimpe is just lucky. That's all." Isioma shook her head, her anger finally cooling. "But abeg, leave Bimrritant alone."

I stopped laughing for a second, raising an eyebrow. "Bim-what?"

"Bimrritant!" Isioma repeated, her face serious as if she had coined the world's most important term. "Bimpe the irritant. That's what she is now."

I shook my head, still laughing. "Isioma! This your mouth… it's too sharp."

She shrugged, clearly unbothered by her newfound nickname for Bimpe.

Thinking of our last conversation about Bimpe, I smiled. I missed my friends; I missed the banter and was looking forward to seeing Isioma when she came home for Christmas.

* * *

The years breezed by, and before we knew it, we were in our final year in the university. As was expected, Aunty Dunni's home had become our regular holiday spot.

Even Halima started joining us there whenever she was in Lagos.

As much as we loved staying at my aunt's glamorous house, there was no way our mothers would let us spend Christmas anywhere else but with them. Halima spent Christmas in Dubai with her family even though they were Muslims, while Isioma headed to the east for the holidays.

So, it was just me, alone with Alaba for Christmas.

This year though, we had a reason to celebrate. Taiye had finally arrived home for the holiday and her engagement, and with her came her white boyfriend, Brian.

Taiye was the sibling we never thought would get married, so Mum was willing to accept anyone she presented—even if it had been a lizard, as she liked to joke. But Brian wasn't just anyone. He was a perfect match for Taiye, who had always been an incredibly careful and perceptive judge of character. If Taiye said someone was good, that person was good, no questions asked. She had a way of understanding people deeply, even before they revealed their true selves.

Brian, with his easy-going charm, won everyone over in minutes. He looked surprisingly comfortable in our traditional attire—a loose white blouse and purple wrapper. His parents, six friends, and his younger sister, Kate, had also dressed in Nigerian clothes. It turned out Kate had been the one to introduce the couple. She and Taiye had formed a close friendship while studying together, and one dinner at Kate's family home had been all it took for Taiye and Brian to click.

The engagement party itself was far from the usual small gatherings Mum liked to host. It was packed. Everyone knew her daughter was back with her 'Oyibo' husband. Dad had wisely suggested we use a hall to avoid the post-party cleanup, and Mum had agreed. Lola couldn't attend as she was heavily pregnant with baby number three, but she had been present for the court wedding in America. Kenny was there, her family in tow, along with Alaba, Mr. and Dr. Adetokunbo, and of course, Labisi, who had somehow convinced her dad to let her come home for the holidays.

In the middle of the chaos, I found myself helping Kenny with her baby Tolani when, without warning, the tiny bundle threw up all over me. I couldn't help but laugh, though Kenny was flustered, as she apologised and I told her not to worry and offered to take the baby upstairs to clean her up as I needed to change too.

On my way into the house with the baby, I met an elderly aunty who wanted to know where I was going. When I told her, she started smiling and saying it was a good omen that I would soon have my own babies. I almost hissed out loud as I wondered if everything a baby did to an adult was a good omen.

By the time I had finished with the baby and cleaned myself up, I heard footsteps approaching the room. I scooped up the baby, ready to leave, when I turned and saw Demola standing in the doorway.

My heart nearly jumped out of my chest. "My goodness! Demola! You scared me," I said, trying to calm my racing heartbeat.

"Sorry," he said, smiling as he walked over and enveloped me, baby and all in a warm hug. "How are you?"

"I... I'm fine." I stammered, still recovering from the shock of seeing him. "When did you get in? How come nobody mentioned you were in town?"

Demola laughed. the sound rich and comforting. "I told them not to mention it. May I?" he asked, motioning to the baby in my arms.

"What?" I asked, momentarily confused.

"Hold the baby. She's Kenny's, right?"

"Yeah," I replied, handing the baby to him. As he took her in his arms, I had a moment to really look at him. He wasn't the same Demola who had left for London. He looked more mature, polished. He was dressed in a white shirt and grey trousers. His black shoes were so shiny I was sure if I leaned down, I'd see my own reflection in them. The sleeves of his shirt were rolled up just enough to show off his well-toned forearms. I wasn't much of a perfume enthusiast, but whatever he was wearing, it was doing things to my senses.

Demola and I hadn't seen much of each other over the years because we missed each other when I was home or when he visited from London.

Without thinking, I reached up and touched his face. His skin was warm beneath my touch, and I felt an electric current pass through me.

"What are you doing?" his voice was low, almost a whisper, pulling me back to reality.

"Touching you," I blurted out, immediately regretting it. My hand snapped back to my side, and I covered my mouth in embarrassment. "Oh my gosh, I'm sorry. I didn't mean to... I don't know what I was thinking."

Demola chuckled, shaking his head slightly. "You don't need to apologize, Mide."

Before I could respond, the door swung open, and there stood Labisi, her usual mischievous grin plastered on her face. "Oh, there you are! The two of you. I was starting to wonder where you'd gone."

I rolled my eyes at the way she said, 'the two of you'. "I'm sure you weren't wondering. You probably followed him up here," I muttered under my breath. Labisi, like Alaba, was the typical nosey little sister.

Demola, still holding the baby, turned to me. "Are you done? We can head back down together."

I nodded, grateful for the escape.

We made our way down the stairs, Labisi trailing behind us with a smile I wished she would wipe off her face.

Kenny spotted us first, when we stepped outside, and broke into a wide grin. "Oh, thank you Mide. Did you take enough photos in your dress?" Kenny said as Demola gently handed her the baby.

"I did." I replied.

I knew she was concerned since I had to change my asoebi, but clothes were not my concern. It was Demola who was standing next to me and who seemed to shadow me throughout that had me captivated. Demola stayed to chat for a bit and then I saw him off after promising him that I would visit when he returned from Abuja.

Chapter Fourteen

It was eight days to Christmas when I got the news that would break my heart.

I was lounging in the living room reading a novel when my dad walked in. The festive season was still in full swing, and though the estate was loud with the usual holiday energy, our home felt quieter than usual. That was because mum and Alaba were having a nap after making some deserts including chin-chin.

He sat down beside me on the couch and gently folded his hands in his lap. He was silent for a few minutes until I looked up at him.

No one needed to tell me something was amiss.

"Mide" He paused.

"Yes dad." I said and immediately sat up and placed the novel on the coffee table before me.

He took a deep breath then shook his head before he continued. By this time, my heart had started racing. My father was never this dramatic. What was the problem? I asked myself.

"I just got off the phone with Halima's mother," Dad began, his voice soft but filled with concern.

I dropped my feet on the floor, immediately alert. "Is everything okay?"

Dad sighed, rubbing the back of his neck. "Halima's not well. Her mum said she's been very sick for a while now. She asked if you and Isioma could come and visit her in Abuja."

My heart sank. Halima, very sick? My dear friend always had the brightest smile and the most infectious laugh, being sick didn't describe her. "Daddy, who told you Halima is sick?" I asked, my voice trembling slightly.

Dad looked at me, his eyes filled with sympathy. "Her mum called me. She didn't go into too much detail, but she said Halima has been asking for you and Isioma. She thinks it would do Halima good to see her friends."

Without hesitation, I got to my feet.

"Please can I ring Isioma? I asked my dad. He nodded and showed me where he dropped his new Nokia handset. I grabbed it and rang Isioma. She was on holiday in Enugu with her family, but she had rung earlier to say she would be in Lagos for the new year.

When she answered, I could hear children playing in the background.

"What's up. Did you hear that Halima isn't feeling well?" I asked without considering that she may not have heard. I kicked myself immediately.

"Yea, but my mum didn't have much information. what's going on?" Isioma's voice immediately became serious.

I explained everything Dad had told me, my voice shaking as I relayed the news. I didn't know why I was shaking.

I just knew that something wasn't right.

"Oh my gosh," Isioma whispered, her voice barely audible. "Do you think it's serious?

"I don't know. I just know she wants us to come."

"We need to go then."

"We do. Her mum said They are in Abuja now. Can you fly out from Enugu?"

Isioma didn't hesitate. "Of course. I'll talk to my mum, and we'll buy a ticket for a flight tomorrow."

"I'll do the same," I said. "See you tomorrow."

We hung up, and I turned to my dad. "Isi's coming too. Can we go tomorrow?"

Dad nodded. "I'll make the arrangements. I will go to Abuja with you."

"Daddy what do you think is wrong?" I asked, even though I wasn't expecting a response different from the one he gave earlier.

"I don't know my dear. We will find out later. "For now, pray for her healing."

I nodded barely able to speak. How serious was this sickness? I didn't like my father's face. He wasn't hiding any information, was he?

The next morning, my dad and I headed to the airport. I had barely slept the night before; my thoughts were consumed by memories of a healthy Halima. One with an infectious laugh and quick wit. The thought of her being sick and wanted us to come and visit her sent a deep ache through me. We fell sick occasionally, and often rang to check on each other, but none of us had ever requested the others to visit.

Maybe this was because we were in different parts of the country.

Isioma's flight landed shortly before ours, so she and her mum chose to wait for us at the airport. Not long after our plane descended, we met them at the departure gate. Isioma looked pale from her worry. We hugged tightly, both of us clinging to each other as if we hadn't seen in years, while our parents talked.

"My spirit feels like something is very wrong." Isioma whispered as we boarded the bus my dad hired to take us to the hospital to see Halima.

"I know," I replied, blinking back tears. "But we're here now, right? Everything will be alright."

The weather in Abuja was warm, almost comforting, but we felt anything but comfort. Halima's father met us at the reception when we got to the hospital and that was when I sensed something was wrong.

He looked exhausted, like someone who hadn't slept in days.

Fear gripped me. What was going on? Why was Halima in the hospital? How serious was this illness? Isioma and I walked behind our parents as we moved through the hospital corridor.

The sterile smell and the amount of sick people we saw were enough to break a persons' spirit. We held hands as we walked trying to listen in on the conversation our parents were having. They spoke in low voices, so it was difficult to hear them. The faint beeping of machines and the smell of antiseptic became stronger as we reached Halima's room.

Her mother was sitting by the door and stood up immediately to greet us. She looked worse than her husband. Her eyes held the tell-tale signs of someone who must have been crying. They were swollen and red.

"Good afternoon aunty." We greeted in union as we went into her open arms.

"My darlings. Thank you for coming," she whispered and managed to give us a soft but sad smile. I felt my heart tighten in my chest.

Suddenly, I couldn't breathe. I squeezed Isioma's hand as if it would give me the air I needed.

"She's been asking for both of you." Aunty Amina said.

I swallowed hard and nodded, trying to keep my emotions in check as she led Isioma and I into the room.

Nothing could have prepared us for what we saw.

Halima lay on the hospital bed, surrounded by machines.

She looked nothing like the vibrant girl we remembered. Her skin was pale, almost translucent, and her frame had become frail, a shadow of the lively girl who used to dance around. Her eyes, once so full of life, now looked tired and heavy with very dark circles around them. Her beautiful Fulani hair she had inherited from her mother was gone, replaced by a very thin scarf.

"Halima?" Isioma whispered, stepping closer to the bed.

Halima's eyes flickered open. Her eyes scanned the room until it landed on us. A faint smile touched her lips. "You made it," she said, her voice weak but it still held its warmth.

I choked back a sob and forced a smile. "Of course we did."

We sat on either side of her bed, holding her hands, trying to be strong. There was no way I was going to spend the most of my time there weeping. I decided to make the most of our time there, though, it wasn't easy. We told her of Taiye's wedding, and that we had brought souvenirs from Lagos for her.

We talked about everything we could remember just so there was no unhappy moment. Halima laughed, at our stories, but even that small act seemed to drain her.

After a while, the exhaustion became too much for her, and she closed her eyes. "I'm so glad you came," she whispered. "I honestly didn't want to trouble you."

"Don't say that. You're never a trouble to us," Isioma said, her voice breaking. I looked at her immediately silently asking her to maintain her composure.

"What's wrong?" Isioma continued as her eyes filled with tears.

Halima smiled.

She moved her hands along the bed one after the other until they reached ours. It was as if she wanted to touch both our hands, so we moved our hands closer.

"I'm sorry." She whispered.

"It's ok." I whispered.

"No, let me talk." She continued to speak. Her breath strained with each word. Taking short deep breath, she said, "I'm dying."

The words shocked us into silence.

"What do you mean?" Isioma asked. The tears she had been trying to hold were flowing like the Niger river now. It was as if a tap had just opened. I simply sat there motionless, unable to speak.

"Isioma, I have cancer."

"Jesus." I finally spoke in the lowest tone.

Halima smiled again, her pain evident. "It's a rare one. My parents will tell you everything."

"Why didn't you tell us?" I asked.

My tears were threatening to fall but I was doing everything to suppress them.

Halima breath was strained. "I didn't want you to worry. Forgive me," she said.

"Halima…" Isioma said. Her words were lost in the tears.

"Shhh…It's okay." Halima said. She sounded so weak. We could hear her wheezing. "It's okay."

"No, it's not. I will pray." I said trying to hold my tears as I lifted a hand to stroke her hair or what was left of it. "We will pray. You're going to get better, and we are going to spend the next holiday with my aunt."

Isioma nodded as if the gesture was an assurance of an already planned holiday.

Again, Halima's smile was weak, but it was there. "Not this time my darlings." She whispered, "Not this time."

"Don't say that." I whispered.

But Halima seemed to have made peace with it. She winced, then she stroked my hand and Isioma's.

"Does it hurt?" Isioma asked between tears.

Halima nodded. "It does. It hurts. I can't manage the pain anymore."

I was trying to control myself, but it wasn't working. Isioma on the other hand was a mess. She was almost wailing.

"Can't they do anything." I asked. My voice was low, and I found it difficult to say the words.

"It will only extend the pain. It won't heal me." Halima whispered. "It's okay my loves. I have accepted my fate, truth be told, I am tired."

I'm sorry." I whispered as Halima closed her eyes again.

Her mother came in then to make her more comfortable before she gently guided us out so Halima could rest.

"Don't forget me." Halima managed to say as we left the room.

"We won't. See you tomorrow, right?" I said, but her words left me broken completely.

As soon as the door closed behind us, the façade of strength I had maintained for her sake shattered. Reaching for Isioma, we clung to each other, tears streaming down our faces as we sobbed quietly in the hallway.

"Why?" Isioma whispered, her voice barely audible. "She doesn't even look like Halima anymore."

"I know," I replied, my heart breaking with each word. "I can't believe this is happening. God please." I prayed

We cried until there were no more tears left. My dad and Halima's dad standing nearby, didn't say much. They couldn't, both men looked helpless and unsure of what to do or say but their presence was a comfort.

Halima's mum came out of the room minutes later.

"My baby is leaving me. Ya Allah…" she fell to the ground weeping. Isioma, her mum and I rushed to her side to comfort her. Her dad stood crossed arms and shaking his head. It was a terrible feeling.

The atmosphere, everything felt suffocating.

"Tomorrow would be better." I said trying to comfort her.

"Insha Allah." She responded nodding multiple times, but tomorrow wasn't any better for that night, Halima left us.

The news came early the next morning. Even though we knew the day would come, nothing could have prepared us for it. It was too soon. We were supposed to visit her that morning.

Isioma and I chose to stay in one room. Nothing could dull the pain we felt inside. I fell to the floor weeping when we were told while Isioma sat on the bed rocking herself as she clutched her legs, resting her chin on her knees.

Halima's parents were inconsolable. We tried to comfort them, but there were no words that could ease the loss of a child. Her mother moved around like a zombie, a complete shadow of herself.

The days that followed Halima's passing moved in a blur.

Everything felt numb as we helped her parents prepare for the funeral. Her mother and father, usually so welcoming and warm, looked hollow now, their faces heavy with grief and exhaustion. Her siblings were no better either; it was as if the light had gone out of their lives. They just sat down in their rooms looking into space.

Isioma and I spent most of our time in their home, answering the door for guests, helping to arrange chairs for visiting relatives, and running small errands. Anything to feel helpful and keep our own hearts occupied.

The night before the funeral, as we sat quietly in the living room with Halima's mother, we wondered how Halima had kept her sickness from us. As though reading our minds, her mother cleared her throat and said quietly.

"I owe you girls an explanation," she said, her voice low and tearful. "About what happened with Halima."

Isioma and I exchanged glances, our eyes filling with tears.

"No, aunty. We understand." I said, looking at her then at Isioma who was crying silently. I wanted her to stop because of Halima's mum, but who was I to determine how people choose to grieve.

Halima's mum smiled and shook her head sadly. "It happened so suddenly," she continued, her voice thick with emotion. "A few months ago, Halima had a simple cold. We didn't think much of it—just something that lingered a bit longer than usual, but it persisted for months." She paused, her voice catching.

We nodded because Halima had mentioned having a strong cold.

Her mum continued to speak. "Her first diagnosis was a cold. They missed it. By the time we realized something was wrong, the doctors told us he had an advanced cancer. A rare form according to the doctor. He said that it had spread silently. They started her on chemotherapy, but she opted out when the pain became too much, and the doctors confirmed she had little to no chance of beating it. She didn't have any symptoms besides having a cold. Nothing that could have warned us or prepared us for this."

Isioma let out a choked sob, quickly covering her mouth. I reached over and took her hand, holding it tightly as we listened. My heart ached for Halima and the silent battle she had fought without telling us, choosing to protect us from the pain she was feeling.

"She didn't want anyone to know," Halima's mother continued, wiping a tear from her cheek. "She asked us not to say anything to her friends. She didn't want you both to worry or be sad, so she kept it from you."

Silence settled over us as we absorbed her words. Finally, Halima's mother took a deep breath, looking at us with very sad eyes and a gentle smile.

"She was so strong. My darling baby girl. Before she passed, she wrote letters to each of you," she said, reaching into her handbag and pulling out two small, carefully folded letters. She handed one to Isioma and the other to me. "She wanted you both to have these. She joked about getting it done before she lost all her strength." A tear finally escaped and slid down her cheek as she spoke.

I took the letter from her hands, feeling its weight as if it held everything Halima had kept in her heart.

My fingers trembled as I carefully unfolded it.

Halima's big and beautiful handwriting filled the page. That was another thing. Halima had the most beautiful handwriting. We always made her sign cards and other things on our behalf. Plus, if you needed to borrow anyone's note, it would be Halima's. It wasn't like we didn't have nice handwritings; Halima's was just out of this world.

As I read the first line of the letter, my vision blurred as tears filled my eyes. This was Halima. No one else spelt my name like she did.

Mee Day my girl!

By the time you read this, I would have gone to be with Allah. Forgive me. I'm sorry for not telling you, for keeping this hidden and for lying about going to Dubai (It was the best I could come up with at the time). I just didn't want you to be sad, to look at me differently, or to look at me the way you do right now. I can see the tears girl, but guess what? It's okay. You and Isi have always been there for me. You both are my friends, my sisters, my partners in everything fun and ridiculous. And in my heart, I still see us that way. I want you to remember me laughing, talking about our silly dreams and secrets. Not like this.

*Please promise me you'll keep smiling, that you'll live the life we always dreamed of. Mide let your prince charming know how you feel about him *wink* Yes girl, I've always known about Demola."*

I froze when I read that part. How had she known? The little witch. I continued reading the letter.

"You just called me a little witch, ba? Ha ha... I know you my darling and that is why I know you will be fine. Take care of yourself. Take care of Isioma, too. I know she will always put up a strong exterior, then cry when no one is watching. You and I know her very well. Remind her that even though I'm gone, I'll always be with you both. Don't let this stop you from being happy, Mide. Don't let it stop you from believing in God. He remains the greatest and knows why these things happen. I'm sure he will permit me to watch over you both. Be happy for me. And know that I love you—always.

Forever yours,

Halima (matar kulikui).

The tears came then, spilling over and soaking into the paper. Even with all she was going through, she still sounded on top of the word.

She wanted us to be happy.

Isioma looked up from her letter; her face streaked with tears, reaching for each other, we cried together, our hands clasped tightly around our letters from Halima. Her mother reached over, patting our hands gently, her own face was wet with silent tears.

"She wanted you to be strong," she whispered. "She wanted you to remember her love, her laughter, not this illness." She gave each of us a kiss on the forehead and left us in the room.

The next day, which was three days after Halima passed, she was laid to rest.

It was a simple funeral. We did our best to honour her wishes. Her family had arranged for a small, intimate service, and the room was filled with people who loved her.

As we watched the process, her male relatives carry her to her final resting place, I remembered Halima's last words.

"Don't forget me."

After the burial, Isioma and I stood together on the balcony at the back of the house watching the sun setting. It looked exceptionally beautiful that day. Almost as if it was reminding us to be hopeful. It gave us a strange sense of peace. Halima had been loved deeply, and she had left us with a parting gift—her words, her love, and her memory. She had left a will as we chose to call it where she left her things to a few people including Isioma and me.

Isioma and I spent the rest of the day with Halima's mum. supporting her in any way we could, listening as she shared more stories about Halima, stories that made us smile through the sadness.

Soom it was time to return home.

We said our goodbyes to Halima's parents and siblings. Promising to keep in touch, to honour her memory, and to always be there for them. I sat next to Isioma on the plane ride back to Lagos as her mum decided to let her go back with us since the plan that year was to spend Christmas in Enugu and the new year in Lagos.

As the plane taxied down the runway, I looked down at Halima's letter in my lap, tracing the words she had written with my finger. We had enjoyed a good friendship. One some people only dreamt of.

"I'm glad we went," Isioma whispered, her voice breaking the silence.

"Me too. It's good that we stayed for the funeral too." I replied, my heart swelling with a bittersweet mix of sadness and gratitude. "Halima would have wanted us there."

Isioma nodded. "I can't believe she's gone Mide."

"I know. Just like that." I agreed. "God the things you allow…" I said shaking my head.

As the plane soared through the clouds moments later. I closed my eyes, letting the tears slip down my face. I couldn't believe we were never going to hear Halima's voice…ever again.

Chapter Fifteen

I took a shower and went to bed as soon as we got home.

For the first time in a long time, my mum appeared to be genuinely touched. Though she gave me some space. The next day, I was sitting in the living room flipping through an old photo album when the doorbell rang. Alaba, always eager to play host, rushed to answer it.

"It's Labisi!" she called out, her excitement evident.

I set the album aside and stood up, brushing my hands down my shorts. As I walked to the door. Labisi was already in the living room looking as elegant as ever in a simple yellow dress. Her warm smile was a welcome sight, though her eyes reflected the sympathy she carried for me.

"Mide," she said quietly, pulling me into a hug.

I hugged her back, the comfort of her presence brought an unexpected wave of emotion as I blinked back the tears in my eyes, trying to stop them from falling.

"I'm so sorry about your friend. I heard about it from Mum. How are you holding up?" she asked.

"I'm trying," I said quietly.

She pulled back but still held onto my shoulders as she studied my face.

"Pele." she said sorry in Yoruba language, and with a small smile. "Be strong, you hear?"

I nodded. It was hard managing people's grief when they spoke with me because the sadness resurfaced instantly.

Together, we sat in the living room. Alaba hurriedly brought us glasses of zobo and some chin-chin, then disappeared to give us privacy.

"I wanted to come earlier, but things have been so busy at home," Labisi said, taking a sip of her drink. "Mum sends her condolences, by the way."

"Thank you," I said, feeling a surge of gratitude for her thoughtfulness.

We talked about Halima for a while, sharing memories and reflecting on the impact she had on my life, in the short time she lived. Labisi listened intently, nodding and offering kind words. She had met Halima just once and loved her immediately. It wasn't difficult to love Halima, she was thoughtful, kind and mature for her age.

"Oh, by the way, Demola's arriving tomorrow," Labisi said casually, setting her glass down on the coffee table.

I looked at her admiring how she *casually* slipped that bit of information in. "Really? Just for the New Year?"

"Yes, oh." she said with a smile. "My dear London life is not easy. He's been working nonstop, so Mum practically begged him to come home for a bit. But I think he also wants an excuse to see everyone."

I tried to play it cool, but I could feel the excitement creeping up my cheeks. For a moment, I forgot all about my sorrows. "That's nice. It'll be good to see him again."

Labisi tilted her head, narrowing her eyes slightly. "It will, won't it?" she said with a teasing lilt to her voice. "You guys and this your… thing."

I rolled my eyes, trying to brush it off. "There's no 'thing,' Labisi. Demola is our brother. *Our brother*. I said emphasizing the words and flicking a hand between us. I wasn't sure why I felt the need to explain, though.

"Sure," she said, drawing the word out as if she didn't believe me. "But I'm sure you know he's been asking about you."

I frowned, my curiosity piqued, causing me to stammer. "Asking about me? Well, that's normal. What did he say, though?"

"Oh, you know," she said with a mischievous grin. "He's been wondering how you're doing, how school's going, things like that."

I wanted to ask why she said that bit of information the way she did, but Alaba reappeared, breaking the moment. "Are you staying for dinner, Labisi?" she asked in her usual cheerful voice.

"No, not tonight," Labisi said, standing up. "But thank you. I just wanted to check on Mide."

"Okay." Alaba answered and went back in.

Still wanting to ask my question, I turned to Labisi, but she placed her glass down on the table and said it was time she went home. I walked her to the door and thanked her for coming as she hugged me goodbye.

"Take care of yourself, Mide. And don't overthink things." she whispered.

I nodded, watching as she walked to the car she came in where it was parked in the compound. Her visit gave me some comfort and hope. It was time I came out of my room and did something productive with myself. Halima wouldn't have wanted me to be sad.

I closed the door and went into the kitchen to get a broom and dustpan.

My room needed deliverance from its untidy state.

***

Christmas morning was different that year.

The usual excitement that accompanied the day was overshadowed by the weight of Halima's absence. Even the vibrant decorations around the house and the Christmas tree felt like they didn't belong. Alaba and I were in the kitchen, helping Mum serve lunch. Mum noticed my quiet demeanour and placed a gentle hand on my shoulder. To be honest, this was one of the very few times my mum showed concern for me.

"Mide," she said with a very gently tone. "Halima would want you to celebrate, you know. She would want you to smile."

I nodded, blinking back the tears that threatened to spill. "I know, Mum. I'm trying."

Mum pulled me into a brief hug. "That's all you can do, my dear. Just take things one step at a time."

Dad walked in then, dressed in a white agbada.

Christmas day was the only day daddy paid special attention to how he dressed. Normally, he would throw on any traditional piece his hands touched. It was only when he went out with our mum that she made sure he put in a little more effort in his outfit. Then again, I think that is a regular feature with men from the Eastern and Naija Delta part of Nigeria. They dressed simple when going out.

Their wealth was seen more in their wives because they spent with no consideration of the pocket.

My dad smiled at me, although there was a tinge of sadness in his eyes. "The food smells amazing," he said, patting my back. "How about we eat in the garden today? The weather is perfect."

It was a fantastic idea because my parents had recently invested in some garden furniture, and no one had tested them besides mum of course.

I nodded again, grateful for the distraction.

Together, we carried the food outside, where Alaba had already set the table close to the mango tree. The sun was warm and the breeze felt cool against my skin and the garden looked amazing.

As we sat down to eat, Alaba, always the chatterbox, filled the silence with stories about her first semester in the university. Her laughter was contagious. The truth is you could never keep a straight face with her around. I found myself smiling, even laughing a little and it wasn't forced at all. It was like a small ray of light piercing through the heavy clouds.

Sometime after lunch, Isioma called to check on me.

Hearing her voice was a comfort and a reminder that I wasn't alone in missing Halima.

"Hello baby!" Isioma said over the phone. "Merry Christmas. How are you doing?"

"Merry Christmas dear," I admitted. "I'm better. How have you been?"

"Good, good. Trying to make the most of this day." Isioma said in a cheerful voice.

"It's strange, celebrating without her. By now, she would have called to collect her food over the phone."

"I know," she said, her voice tinged with sadness. "But she's watching us, you know. Probably rolling her eyes at us for being so gloomy."

* * *

After lunch I decided to pay Demola a visit.

He had flown in from London, last night and the first thing he did was call me.

Pulling on a large jeans jacket, I walked the short distance to his house and was about to press the bell, when the door swung in and he stood there grinning.

"About time! I was about to come and get you." He said pulling me into a hug. "I am so sorry about Halima, Mide. How is Isioma doing?"

"She's fine, can we not talk about Halima today please?" I whisper, as we stay in each other's arms for a while before he pulled away and pulled me into the house closing the door behind me.

"Okay we won't."

"Is Aunty in?" I asked.

"No, they went out, Daddy's friend is hosting them today, I decided to stay home and wait for you."

"You were very sure I would come" I asked quietly as I slid off my jeans jacket.

"Yeah, we can just hang here a while," he said, trying to sound casual.

Was I wrong to sense there was something else in his tone?

I raised an eyebrow. "What, and miss all the fun in my house?" I teased, trying to lighten my own nervous energy.

He shrugged, flashing me a playful grin. "Or we could make our own fun here, no?"

I tilted my head, wondering what he meant, but he simply gestured towards his flat-screen and the stack of video games. "A little FIFA, maybe?"

I laughed, feeling my nerves ease. "Not a bad idea, but first, could I have a shirt or something? This jacket is too thick, and I didn't think to change the top I was wearing before I left the house," I admitted, tugging at my tight tank top that clung to my breast.

His eyes widened as he glanced down at my chest, then he looked away quickly. "Oh, right! Sorry, love. Let me get you something suitable, hang the jacket on the rack."

Love.

The word slipped out of his mouth so casually, yet it sent my heart racing. My mind scrambled over the word, overanalysing it, wondering if he meant anything by it as I followed him to his room.

Demola walked up to his closet rummaging through it before he finally handed me a large, soft snoodie.

"This is large!" I said looking at it.

'Trust me, it's better than what you have on." He answered.

"But how do you wear it in this heat?" I wanted to know because the snoodie was large.

"I don't. I use it mostly in winter, when I travel." He said smiling.

"Oh!" I said feeling foolish. Of course he did. I turned and walked into his bathroom to change. It felt a bit strange getting changed in his bathroom, but I loved the feeling. The snoodie smelled like Demola. I pulled it gently over my head, the oversized sleeves practically swallowed me whole, but I didn't mind. It was like a cocoon.

I emerged from the bathroom minutes later smiling shyly. "Thanks," I said, pulling the sleeves over my hands for extra warmth.

Demola gave me an approving nod. "Looks good on you," he said.

His eyes did not leave mine and I could feel a blush creeping up my cheeks, so I quickly looked away, feigning interest in the game controllers on his bed. "So, FIFA?"

He chuckled as he grabbed a controller and sat down on the edge of the bed.

"Okay," he said rubbing his hands still holding the controller. "Be warned, I don't go easy on anyone."

"Oh, please," I scoffed, picking up the other controller and sitting beside him. "You're not that good."

"Oh, you'll see," he said, smirking and leaning just a little too close, so his knee brushed mine.

Soon we fell into a rhythm, caught up in the game, teasing and nudging each other, laughing at every missed shot or goal scored. The cozy room felt like our own little world, shut off from the world outside. I was so absorbed in the game and the warmth of his snoodie that I forgot about thoughts of Halima that had shadowed me all day.

About half an hour later, as the second game threatened to end in a draw, I scored a goal out of nowhere, then the final whistle went. I threw my arms up in victory, grinning widely. "Yes! Finally! I told you I'm not that easy to beat."

Demola groaned, tossing his controller onto the bed in mock defeat. "Alright, alright. I'll admit it—for now."

Our laughter faded, and I realized just how close we were sitting. Our knees were still touching, and he was watching me, more intensely. For a moment there, the light-hearted atmosphere shifted to an electric one that made my heart pound.

"You're full of surprises, you know," he said in a whisper, his eyes never leaving mine.

The weight of it all made my breathing faster. His face was close—so close I could see the way his jaw tensed just slightly. Meanwhile my heart thundered in my chest, and I knew he could probably feel my nervous energy, but I couldn't look away.

His gaze flickered down to my lips, and then back up to my eyes, and I was certain, I could hear my pulse. My heart was going to explode. My entire body was aware of the little space between us. Was this really happening? Was he finally going to kiss me? That would mean I was his type of girl, wouldn't it?

Oh God I prayed, let it happen.

He lifted his hand to trace my lips before looking up at me.

"Mide…" he whispered.

I was quiet but I could feel my heart pounding as he traced my lips with his finger, his eyes locked onto mine and then he moved and finally his lips were on mine.

My eyes shot up in surprise, as he pulled back to look at me, unsure of my reaction and then with a groan, he moved and covered my lips with his. I didn't need to think twice, as my mouth opened underneath his, and his tongue swept into my mouth.

Oh God! Demola was kissing me, and it felt so good, and I was kissing him back, a moan escaped from my throat as he moved, lifting me to place me across his laps never breaking the kiss.

He kissed me like he could never get enough of me.

Kissed me like it mattered and when I shuddered, he broke the kiss to lean his forehead against mine.

"God Mide, the things you make me want to do to you." He whispered.

I couldn't speak, my heart was pounding I was sure it would explode in my chest, Demola had kissed me, he had kissed me, finally!

"Mide?"

"I have to go now!" I say, scrambling to get off him not before I see the disappointed look on his face. As I stood, looking anywhere but at him.

Finally, he stood, his movements hesitant as if he, too, was reluctant to break the moment. "We should probably head back down before Labisi and my folks return" he said, quietly.

"Yeah, I think I will just go home" I replied, dazed, feeling like I was walking in a dream.

He nodded, disappointed, taking a step back he nodded towards the door, waiting for me to lead the way out. I didn't walk, I ran with my jacket as soon as we got downstairs and before Demola could say another word, I was out of the house and running down the driveway.

Chapter Sixteen

One would think now that Demola had proven he was attracted to me, I would be happy, no! I was in a panic whenever I thought about the kiss, and yes, I began avoiding him. I knew I was being childish but how do you handle it, when your childhood crush finally makes a move on you.

Nothing!

You run as fast as your legs can carry you before you make a fool of yourself.

I couldn't avoid Demola for long as his father fell ill and my Mum insisted that we all visit Aunty Amaka from time to time to offer our support. Demola had postponed his trip, intending to wait till his father was better before he returned to work.

God help me, I couldn't stop thinking of that kiss and how I had felt when his lips touched mine, I ran because I was scared, my memory of intimacy is not very good, so it was no surprise I became scared the first time a man touched me after my horrible experience.

Even if the man was Demola.

To my embarrassment, my dreams had escalated from kissing Demola to smooching with him and I was going crazy knowing, he had stopped asking of me after he realised, I was avoiding him.

But things came to a head one day, when Mum asked me to drop off stew, she had made for Aunty Amaka, one afternoon. When I got to their house, the maid informed me, that Labisi had accompanied her Mum to the hospital.

"Brother Demola is upstairs, though," she added, casually.

"Demola is around?" I asked her. "He didn't go with Labisi to the hospital."

"No ma, he is upstairs." She replied. "I'm heading to the market now," the maid continued. "Are you staying, ma? Should I lock the door, or would you like me to leave the key?"

"Yes, I'll stay," I replied, taking the key from her, I was already here, and it would be childish for me to just leave when I knew he was upstairs. "I'll lock up after you."

I waited for her to leave, then I locked the door behind her and made my way upstairs to Demola's room. I knocked, but there was no response. I knocked again, but still nothing. Hesitating only slightly, I gently turned the doorknob and stepped inside, closing the door behind me, before I turned round.

You know when people say, your village people are looking for you to punish you?

This was one of those times.

Or how else would I explain the fact, I walked into the room at the exact moment that Demola emerged from the bathroom, completely naked, with nothing but a small towel in his hand. My heart dropped all the way to my feet as my breath caught in my throat.

I felt my body go warm all over as our eyes met. I know I should have looked away or turned and left the room, but I couldn't move. My eyes followed the towel as it slowly traced over his well-toned, muscular body, catching droplets of water from his chest down to his stomach and then, Jesus, the guy was loaded down there.

When had he become so... beautiful?

I had always thought Demola was attractive, but now, standing in front of me, he looked like a man completely transformed. He had clearly been working out, his biceps and abs were sculpted, his skin smooth and glistening with water.

He was... breathtaking.

And then, he stopped my thoughts.

"Enjoying the show?" His voice, deep and amused, broke through my trance.

My head shot up in embarrassment.

"Jesus, Jesus, Jesus." I said in a whisper clearly embarrassed. Oh God, he had caught me staring. I didn't know what to say. I was rooted to the spot for some seconds before my feet finally found the will to move, and I turned to leave, but before I could take another step, he caught my arm.

"Don't go," Demola said in the sexiest voice I had heard. Why was it sexy though? Was it because I had just seen him naked? The revelation sent shivers down my spine.

"I.." was all I could manage in a whisper. I couldn't even bring myself to look at him. Despite being tall for a girl, Demola towered over me, making me feel small in his presence. Plus, I was ashamed of myself.

I had been caught staring at him.

"Look at me," he whispered. "Mide... look at me."

I raised my eyes slowly, but the heat in his gaze made me look away again, my cheeks burning.

"Do I make you uncomfortable?" His voice was low, almost teasing, but there was a seriousness in his question.

"Yes, I, I mean, no. I..." I stammered, feeling completely out of my depth.

He chuckled, his deep voice sent shivers down my spine. Slowly, he lowered the towel just enough to cover himself, a gesture that somehow only made the situation more intense, because I was aware of what he was doing. "Come," he said.

Once again, it wasn't a request, it was more of a command, and before I knew it, I found myself following him to the bed. He guided me to like a child; his hand held onto mine as if to steady me. A moment later, I watched in silence as he walked butt naked across the room, his broad back rippling with each movement. He retrieved a larger towel from his closet, then loosely wrapped it around his waist before turning back to face me.

"Is this better?" he asked, flashing me a disarming smile.

Did he know the effect his smile had on me?

I felt my heart had stopped functioning. Where was it because I couldn't feel it? I couldn't breathe too. Was I fighting against his body or my own heart?

"Y-yes," I whispered, my voice barely audible.

"You're sure you're okay, Mide?" He sat down beside me on the bed. I asked myself why he did that as his closeness made it even harder to think straight.

I swallowed hard, forcing myself to respond. "I... I should leave." But I didn't move.

"Is being here with me so bad Mide?" he asked.

I couldn't. Instead, I found myself drawn to him in a way I couldn't explain.

My eyes traced his lips, and without thinking, I licked my own nervously. His gaze darkened at the movement, and before I could fully comprehend what was happening, he bent his head and kissed me.

"*Praise God!*" my shameless inner voice screamed.

His lips brushed mine in the softest and gentlest kiss. It was like a spark igniting something deep inside me, as heat that spread through my body. The kiss didn't last long though. He pulled back slightly, his eyes searching mine, as if asking for permission to continue. My heart pounded in my chest, my breath coming in shallow gasps. Something tightened like a fist in my gut moving lower to the part between my legs.

I didn't know what to say, but my body did.

I came to a quick decision.

Slowly, I lifted my hand, curling my fingers around the back of his neck, and pulled him closer. He groaned softly. This time, when our lips met, there was no hesitation. He closed his eyes, and I did the same. The kiss deepened, and I felt myself melting into him, lost in the sensation of his mouth against mine. His hands found their way to my waist, pulling me closer until I was pressed against his chest, feeling the heat of his skin through the thin fabric of the towel.

Somewhere in the back of my mind, I knew I should stop. This was Demola—my friend, practically my brother. We were not supposed to be doing this, but in that moment, it didn't matter. Nothing else mattered except the way his lips felt against mine, the way his hands moved over my body, the way he made me feel alive in a way I had never felt before.

Demola was the only man I had ever kissed. Nobody had come that close, and the much I remembered about the night I was attacked, there had been no kissing. It was still a painful memory but the fact that I could share something with Demola, blocked the whole episode away.

He lifted me effortlessly, as if I weighed nothing, laying me down on the bed as he kissed me again. His hands moved with deliberate care, exploring the curves of my body as if he were memorizing every inch of it. I didn't want him to stop. I didn't want the moment to end.

Just when I thought my brain was going to explode, he pulled back gently.

"Mide," he whispered, his voice thick with desire, even I didn't recognise it. "I'll stop if you want me to, but don't think I can do that on my own. Just say the word and I will stop." He said staring deep into my eyes.

Say the word, how? What was going on? No, I didn't want him to stop. I wanted more, more of him, more of this feeling, more of everything. I flexed my hips, shifting slightly to bring myself in line with his arousal. We both gasped when I felt it. I gripped the back of his neck again and pulled him down while I raised my head to meet his kiss. Just before our lips met, he stopped and asked me again if, I was sure.

"I want you," I whispered, the words slipping out before I could stop them.

"There's no going back from here babe." He said with a little pause, looking deep into my eyes, as if searching for any hesitation. When he found none, he lowered his head and kissed me again, this time with more urgency, more need. He made a low growl as he parted my lips with his tongue. He tasted so good. I wasn't a good kisser, and I never had a boyfriend. If I was terrible, Demola didn't indicate so I guessed he didn't mind.

I pulled him closer when he started unbuttoning my shirt. I had on a new set of underwear Taiye just sent to me from America and I hoped that would impress him. It did. He lifted his head when he was done with my buttons and looked down at my breasts still clad in my lace bra. I felt shy and tried to cover them with my arm, but he stopped me as he reached behind me to unclasp my bra and tossed it on the floor.

"Don't. You're beautiful." He whispered. Slowly, he kissed the top of each breast then moved up to my throat and captured my mouth in a kiss that rendered me completely senseless.

Demola kissed me like a hungry man.

My entire body was on fire. To be honest, I can't remember when he took off the rest of my clothes. I just knew I was naked when he parted my thighs with his leg. In slow movements, he kissed me making a trail from my mouth to my neck then he moved down kissing the mounds of my breast.

My brain nearly exploded when he took one of my nipples in his mouth and began sucking, while his fingers played with the other one. Then he switched to the other nipple sucking it, before he kissed his way down my stomach, parting my legs, he planted light kisses on my thighs and flicked his tongue against me causing me to buck against him, before he finally took me in his mouth.

I bucked as my world exploded.

I whimpered softly as I held onto his head, buried deep, between my thighs.

I screamed out loud as he kissed, licked and sucked me, driving me over the edge. My body trembled with the force of my release, and my legs went limp as he kissed his way back up to capture my mouth in a searing kiss.

His hands moved parting my legs and finally, when he slid into me, it was a pleasure I could not describe.

Every touch, every kiss, every movement was filled with a wild energy that left me breathless as we came together in wild passion. Demola kissed me and held me close as he emptied himself into me, all the while calling my name repeatedly.

After that, we drifted off to sleep with his strong arms wrapped around me protectively. I rested my head against his chest, listening to the steady rhythm of his heartbeat, feeling more at peace than I had in a long time.

At that moment, I knew we had crossed the bridge of friendship and attraction into whatever it was we were now. Things would never be the same between us. Perhaps we would wake up to the realisation that we just made a mistake, or maybe not. Honestly, I was content just being there with him, in that moment, where everything felt right.

* * *

A loud, piercing sound jolted me awake.

I sat up quickly, my hands pressed against my chest, trying to calm the frantic rhythm of my heartbeat. For a moment, I couldn't figure out where I was, panic set in, but then it didn't take long, like a tidal wave, the memories came rushing back.

Oh, my goodness!

I glanced down at myself.

I was naked, wrapped in sheets that didn't belong to me, in a bed that wasn't mine. My eyes widened as the realisation hit me. It wasn't a dream, Demola and I had been intimate, not once, not twice, multiple times.

The first time could have been excused as a mistake, a lapse in judgment but the second time... the second time had been deliberate.

Intentional.

I had wanted it so badly.

My heart pounded harder. I had to leave. I couldn't stay here, not after what had just happened. How could I even look at Demola now? How could I face him after... after everything? My skin still tingled from his touch, from the way his hands had moved over me, teaching me things about my body, about things I hadn't even known I wanted to learn. I blushed deeply at the memory of it all, of the things we had done and the things I had let myself try.

I had to leave.

I turned to slip out of the bed as quietly as possible, but Demola stirred beside me. His arm shot out, catching me by the wrist and pulling me back down beside him.

His grip was gentle, but it held me in place.

"Don't go," he whispered, his voice still thick with sleep. "Please, don't go."

I froze.

His words were soft and pleading.

The warmth of his body pressed against mine wasn't helping, and for a second, I wanted to stay, I wanted to lie back down and let everything fade away but I couldn't. stay, I had to leave.

I couldn't face him—not now, maybe not ever.

He would wake up soon, and when he did, he would regret everything that had happened between us. He would realise that I wasn't the girl he thought I was. Demola would lose all respect for me, I'm sure he had already.

Oh God! I could still feel his lips and hands all over me. The things he had taught me, the things I tried and the stuff he had done to me.

I blushed at the memory of it all.

Gently, I pulled away from his grasp, slipping out of the bed as quietly as I could. Demola murmured something incoherent, still half asleep, but he didn't stop me this time. I took a deep breath and began searching for my clothes, my heart racing with every passing second.

My panties were under his head, my bra was halfway under the bed, and my top lay crumpled on the floor. Once I had everything on, I tiptoed to the door, holding my breath, praying that no one was around. The house was eerily quiet, and thankfully, there was no sign of anyone as I crept down the stairs. My mind raced as I thought about how I could sneak out without being seen. The last thing I needed was for anyone to ask me questions. Questions I wasn't ready to answer.

Quickly, I slipped out of the house, pulling the door shut behind me as quietly as I could.

The cool breeze hit my face and granted me a sense of relief.

Then I ran.

I ran all the way home.

My feet pounded against the pavement and my breath came in quick, sharp bursts as I raced through the streets. I didn't stop until I reached our front door, unlocking it trembling hands, hands I slipped inside, closing the door behind me with a soft click.

Leaning against the door, I pressed my palms to my face.

Once again, the same thoughts flooded my mind.

How was I going to look him in the eyes after this? I had ruined everything. The connection we had, the friendship that had meant so much to me, was now tangled in new complications. Guilt weighed down on me like a lead blanket as I relived the memories in my head. With a heavy heart, I slipped upstairs to my room and closed the door behind me. I collapsed onto my bed as the events of the day replayed in my mind. There was no way I could block it from my mind as hard as I tried.

The memories had taken over.

I had slept with Demola.

And now I couldn't face him again.

Not after this.

Chapter Seventeen

For days, I couldn't stop replaying everything that had happened with Demola in my mind. What I prayed for had finally led me to where I was now.

I had made a mistake; one I wasn't ready to face but God help me, I couldn't stop thinking of his mouth on me, doing things to me that had driven me crazy.

So, I did the only thing I could think of, which was my usual way of dealing with issues concerning Demola.

I avoided him.

It wasn't easy, but I was determined.

I avoided answering the house phone in case he rang the house. I also ignored the messages he sent through Alaba. They weren't anything serious, just questions about how I was and asking anyone going to our house to say hello to me. I knew he was trying to reach me. He was probably wondering if I wanted to talk. But I couldn't. I couldn't hear his voice without remembering the way it had sounded in the quiet of his room, the way he whispered my name, the way he held me as he made love to me.

I busied myself with studying, trying to keep my mind off everything, but the more I pushed away thoughts of Demola, the more they seemed to surface.

I couldn't shake the feeling that I had ruined everything by sleeping with him and then avoiding him.

One afternoon, Alaba caught me staring blankly at my textbook, my pen motionless in my hand.

"You've been acting strange lately," she said, her eyes narrowed in suspicion as she stood in the doorway of my room. "Are you sure everything's okay?"

I forced a smile, hoping it didn't look as fake as it felt. "I'm fine, just tired. Exams are draining me."

She tilted her head, clearly unconvinced. "You are sure it's just exams? Mide, it's a new semester, isn't it?

"Well, I like to be ahead." I responded.

You still have a week before it begins. Take it easy oh." She said, looking at me as if she suspected more. "Are you sure you are, okay?"

I quickly shut my textbook, trying to deflect. "Yes, Alaba, I am fine."

"Hmm, I don't believe you." She argued in a very low tone.

I didn't even have the strength for an argument. I love my sister, but at that point, she was constituting a nuisance. "I am just focused on school Alaba."

She held my gaze for a moment longer before she shrugged. "Okay ooo, if you say so. But if you need to talk about anything..."

"I know, thanks," I said, cutting her mid-sentence, and at the same time grateful she didn't push further.

As soon as she left, I let out a sigh of relief.

I had a week left of my holiday before returning to school. I was still dodging Demola at every turn. If I knew he was at home, I made sure to be anywhere but there. When I couldn't avoid just being at home, I stayed in my room, pretending to be too busy to come out. Demola as well seemed bent on seeing me. He kept coming over to our house at every opportunity.

The more he came around, the more I did my best to avoid him.

But it was exhausting. And it wasn't fair, to him or to me.

The breaking point came one evening when I was helping Mum with dinner. I was stirring the pot of stew when Mum turned to me, wiping her hands on a dish towel.

"Mide, have you spoken to Demola recently?"

The question hit me like a punch to the gut. I froze, my hand gripping the spoon a little too tightly. "Um, no... not really," I mumbled, hoping she wouldn't notice the tension in my voice.

"He's been asking after you," she said, her tone casual but curious. "Amaka told me he's been worried about you."

"Why?" I asked avoiding not looking at her.

"Why what?" Mum asked.

"Why is he worried?" I asked still avoiding her eyes.

Mum looked at me for a bit before she spoke. "I assume it's because Alaba mentioned to him you were struggling with schoolwork, and he offered to help...like he has always done."

My stomach twisted. Of course, he would be worried, who wouldn't be, after the girl you had mind blowing sex with ghosted you? How could I face him after everything? How could I look him in the eyes when I wasn't even sure how I felt?

Mum watched me closely, her brow furrowing slightly. "Is something wrong, Mide? Aren't you both still close?"

"Yes, we are. I just... I need some time on my own to study, that's all" I said quietly, still not meeting her eyes. "University can be complicated."

"Or have you have finally overgrown your crush?" mum chuckled.

I froze.

Crush?!

How many others knew Demola was my crush? She didn't push further, but the conversation left a heavy weight on my chest. I couldn't keep running from him. I couldn't keep pretending everything was fine when it clearly wasn't.

Later that night, as I lay in bed staring up at the ceiling, I decided. I needed to get away. Not forever, just long enough to clear my head, to figure out what I wanted, what I felt. The only place I could think of was Aunty Dunni's house. Her home had always been a sanctuary, a place where I could escape the pressures of everything else.

After seeking my mum's permission to use her new phone, I sent my aunt a quick text:

"Good evening aunty, can I come and stay with you for a few days? I just need a little break."

Her response came almost instantly:

"Evening my darling. Of course. Come whenever you're ready. My door is always open."

I deleted the messages not wanting her to read our messages.

Sometimes, I felt my mum envied the relationship her children had with her sister who was closer to most of us than she was.

On my way upstairs, I passed Granny's room which had been moved to the ground floor because of her weak knees. I decided to poke my head through the door just to check on her.

"Granny good evening." I greeted through the open door.

"Mide?" she called out as if she wanted to confirm who it was that came in.

"Yes granny." I said as I walked to her bed to kiss her on her baby-like cheeks then sit beside on the bed facing her.

"This one you have finally come to my room, does it mean you are better now?" granny asked.

I chuckled. "How granny?"

"Aah, I don't know my child, but I feel it has to do with Amaka's son." Granny said. She continued to stare into my eyes as if she was looking for a reaction and she got one.

My granny was one person that could sense when anyone in the house had problems. I always admire how she never interfered until you came to her. As for her last comment, it floored me completely. I didn't expect her to be specific.

Granny smiled when she noticed my expression change.

"I don't know what happened but don't fight with him oh. Demola really likes you." She said patting my hands on my laps.

I bent my head focusing on my hands. It was at the tip of my tongue to cry to her, but I held myself.

"Granny I offended him, and I don't think he will forgive me." I said feeling the weight of my comment. I mean, it was the only thing I could come up with. I could have just danced around her comment, but my insides felt like crying. I needed to speak to someone and the only person I could talk about an issue of this magnitude was the person I wanted to escape from.

Granny laughed. "Who? Demola Adetokunbo? Mide that boy can never hold a grudge against you. Don't you know that?" She asked looking at me like I was silly.

"Granny, I don't know oh. I really don't know."

"Omo mi. my child, you don't have a problem. Have you eaten? She asked, suddenly changing the conversation.

"No." I answered.

"Ehen! That one is a problem. Oya go and eat, you hear? The woman was something else. I laughed hard when she said that, and that was how my mum found us. As usual, she remembered something she wanted me to do for her, but granny and I knew better.

"Good night granny." I said as I gave her a hug.

"Good night my dear. Remember what I said." Mum saw her wink at me. As soon as we shut the door to granny's room, mum started her investigation.

"What is going on?"

"What?" I asked feigning innocence.

"You and your granny. Why did she wink at you? What is going on?" she asked again.

"Nothing mum, granny and I were just catching up. I said and walked away from her, but not in a way that would be termed disrespectful.

***

The next morning, I told Mum I needed a change of scenery.

She didn't ask too many questions, just nodded and said she understood. By noon, I was at Aunty Dunni's house. I spent the next few days trying to relax, enjoying the quiet life at Aunty Dunni's. But no matter what I did, even if it was to lay by the pool or to sit on the porch reading, my thoughts kept drifting back to Demola.

I couldn't escape him, not really.

I found out from Alaba that, Demola left for London a few days after I came to Aunty Dunni. He didn't reach out to me before he left, and even though I was the one who created the distance between us, it hurt.

I knew I couldn't stay hidden forever not with how close our families were.

I would see him again at some point, and hopefully when I did, I would finally find the courage to talk to him, to figure out what came next.

And to find out if we had a future together.

CHAPTER eIGHTEEN

"You are pregnant Madam."

The doctor's words echoed in my mind, repeating like a broken record.

"Are you talking to me sir?" I asked confused as I looked up from my test result.

"Yes, Madam." The doctor confirmed

Pregnant? Could my life get any worse than it already was. How could I get pregnant for Demola just like that?

"How far gone am I?" I asked Dr Popoola quietly.

"Nine weeks." Was his reply and it sent shock waves through me.

Nine what?

How had I not known? How had I missed something so life-changing? What was I going to do? How was I going to face my parents? My mother?! Lord what was I going to do?

"Are you ok Madam?" the doctor asked quietly as I gripped the table before me hard.

I nodded absentmindedly, as I got to my feet. "I am, I just need a few minutes to come to term with the news you have given me."

The doctor's concerned voice faded into the background as I mumbled something and left his office. The world outside felt too loud, too bright, contrasting starkly with the numbness that had taken over me.

My thoughts ran wild.

What would I tell my parents? My father's family had always been quick to judge us, they were always waiting for a reason to criticise my Mum, saying she hadn't raised us right.

And now, this… Pregnant.

I clicked my fingers over my head trying to reject the situation.

I Mide Omatseye, almost 21 years old, about to graduate from a Christian university is pregnant.

I knew what this would mean for my family. The shame, the judgment. I could already hear the whispers and disapproving looks. And my school? How could I possibly continue my education? The university had strict rules about morality, and if they found out, I would lose everything my degree, my future, my reputation.

Ah, judgement day had come early.

What would Demola say if I called him and told him, he was going to be a father?

He would have been the one I would normally confide in, but he was off-shore, unreachable for the next few months. The one time we had spoken, it had been awkward, we both knew something had changed but neither of us wanted to acknowledge it.

None of us mentioned that day at his house. It was as if it never happened. He asked me how I was three times in that short conversation, and all I could say was, "I'm fine."

"What was I going to do?" I asked myself.

I took a deep breath, trying to calm the storm inside me. I needed to think. I needed to figure this out before everything came crashing down.

* * *

As I walked through the streets, my phone felt like a heavy weight in my hand. I needed to talk to someone, but who? My thumb hovered over Isioma's contact on my screen, hesitating. She also had a mobile phone now.

I could always count on her to help me through difficult times.

After a deep breath, I pressed the call button. The ringing echoed in my ears, each second stretching out longer than the last.

"Hello, beautiful!" Isioma's bright voice crackled through the phone, bringing a small wave of relief. "What's up? How are you doing?"

I hesitated, my throat tight. How was I supposed to say this? "Hey, Isi," I managed to say, my voice sounding weaker than I intended. "I'm… I'm okay."

There was a brief pause on the other end, and then her voice softened. "You don't sound okay though. What's up?"

I bit my lip, glancing around as if the people walking by could somehow hear the secret, I was trying so hard to keep. "I just… I needed to hear a friendly voice, I guess."

"What's wrong?" she asked again. This time her voice was full of concern. I didn't respond so she continued. "Hello, Mide, what's going on?"

"Isi?"

"Yes Mide?"

"I am pregnant."

Isioma was quiet for a moment, then she said quietly. "Where are you?"

I swallowed hard, trying to shake off the heaviness that clung to me, "I just left the clinic, and I am about to head home."

There was a pause, and then Isioma let out a sigh. "I am coming to yours, say nothing, do nothing, we will figure this out together." She muttered and then she cut the call.

* * *

I was grateful for Isioma.

She came with her father's driver, bundling me into the car. As we drove, she leaned close and said, "We're going to see Aunty Dunni."

"Why?" I asked, though I already dreaded the answer.

"Hmm, apart from Demola's mum, who is in London, Aunty Dunni is the only person I know who can talk to your folks. Or do you plan to keep this a secret forever?"

I nodded. She was right, but a part of me wished I could hide it all.

When we arrived, Aunt Dunni was home and surprised to see us. "Ah ah, Isioma! Mide! How are you both?" she exclaimed, ushering us into the kitchen. "I'm making efo riro. I hope you're hungry. Isioma, will you turn the amala for us? I love how you do it."

"Yes, Aunty," Isioma replied with her easy smile. "But first, Mide has something to tell you."

My stomach dropped. This was the moment I had been dreading.

"Ah, Mide, kilode?" Aunty asked, placing her phone on the table and fixing me with her curious eyes.

Slowly, I reached into my pocket and pulled out the folded paper from the doctor's office. My fingers trembled as I handed it to her.

She sighed as she unfolded it, but the moment her eyes scanned the result, her face paled.

"Mo gbè!" she cried, her hands flying to her head. "I'm finished! Who is pregnant?"

Her dramatic reaction almost made me laugh, despite the weight pressing down on my chest.

"Mide… who is pregnant?" she asked again, searching my face as if praying the paper had lied.

I raised my hand.

Her eyes widened further. "Mo gbè! Mide! How? Ta ni ó fi lóyún? Who is responsible? Your mother will kill me!"

"Aunty, please," I murmured, exhaustion sinking into my bones. "I need your help."

"Help ba wo? How? Who?" she pressed, her voice sharp with urgency.

I hesitated, my mind racing. I couldn't tell her about Demola—not yet. "I'd rather not say right now," I whispered.

"You'd rather not say? Ṣé o ya? Are you sane?" she demanded, staring at me in disbelief.

"Aunty, please. Not now," I begged, my throat tight. Demola didn't even know yet.

"Aah… you're protecting him," she said, softer now but still incredulous. "Is it someone at school? Someone we know?"

I stayed silent. My face gave nothing away, though inside, I was unravelling.

"If you want my help, Mide, you must tell me something," she urged, her tone firm but compassionate.

I swallowed hard. She was right. She deserved to know. But I wasn't ready—not until I'd spoken to Demola.

Her eyes narrowed, then she asked, carefully, "Were you raped?"

The question slammed into me like a blow. "No!" I shouted, louder than I intended. "How can you ask me that?"

"Calm down," she said quickly, though her eyes still searched mine. "I just needed to ask."

"I wasn't, Aunty. That's not what happened." My voice was steadier now, but my heart was racing. "Please… just help me. I promise I'll tell you everything soon."

She studied me for a long moment, then sighed. "Hmmm, Mide…"

"Please, Aunty," I whispered again.

Isioma reached across the table then, squeezing my hand. "Aunty, we came because she trusts you. She's scared. She needs you on her side."

The words seemed to soften Aunty Dunni. She shook her head slowly, still overwhelmed, but her voice gentler now. "Alright. Do your parents know you're here?"

"No, they don't. That's why we came."

Silence stretched between us, broken only by the bubbling pot on the stove. Finally, Aunty Dunni nodded.

"Okay. We will face this together. But Mide…" she leaned closer, lowering her voice, "…this secret cannot hide for long. Be ready."

Isioma's grip on my hand tightened. And for the first time since I had discovered I was pregnant, I let myself breathe.

* * *

The drive home, felt like a funeral procession.

Isioma sat beside me in the backseat, her hand resting lightly on mine, steady and warm, a reminder that she was there for me, while Aunty Dunni rode in front with the driver, a frown on her face.

When we pulled into the compound, my heart thudded so loudly I was certain everyone could hear it. The familiar sight of our gate, the hibiscus flowers my mother loved so much, suddenly looked foreign, ah I felt like I was walking into a lion's den, which I was, when you had a mother like mine that was always quick to judge me.

Inside, my parents were in the sitting room.

My father reading the newspaper, my mother adjusting the curtains. They looked up as we entered, their faces brightening in surprise.

"Dunni! What a pleasant surprise," my mother said, her smile wide. "And you brought Isioma and Mide. Ẹ kú abọ̀."

"Ẹ kú ìrọ̀lé oo," Aunty Dunni greeted politely, bowing slightly.

Isi greeted, then I followed. Her voice was steady, but mine trembled with each word. "Good evening, Daddy. Good evening, Mummy."

"Ah, our children," my mother said warmly, pulling me into a quick embrace before turning to Isioma. "Isioma, it's been so long since I saw you! You've grown even more beautiful."

Isioma smiled shyly. "Thank you, Ma"

For a fleeting moment, everything felt normal but then reality intruded when Aunty Dunni cleared her throat.

"We need to talk," she said, her voice firm, cutting through the pleasantries like a knife.

At once, the atmosphere changed.

"Talk about what?" my father asked, his tone cautious.

Aunty Dunni glanced at me, then back at them. "It concerns Mide."

My father lowered his newspaper as my mother's smile faltered.

"What about Mide?" my father asked, his tone cautious.

Aunty Dunni said quietly. "She's pregnant.

If tension was a person, it would be the perfect description of the atmosphere in the living room. It was thick. I could see the disbelief etched on my mother's face as she looked from Aunty Dunni to me, her eyes opened wide in shock, disbelief.

She repeated my aunt's words slowly, as if saying them out loud would change their meaning.

"She is pregnant. Dunni did you say Mide is pregnant?"

"Sister mi, she is please calm down and let's talk." Aunt Dunni pleaded, trying to get my Mum to look at her

My mother froze, her hands clutched against her chest and then she screamed, a sharp, piercing sound that echoed through the house.

Moments later, Titi, the house help, rushed in, pushing Granny's wheelchair. Granny's face was lined with worry as her eyes darted from my weeping mother to my trembling frame.

"What is going on here?" she demanded, her voice thin but strong for her age. "Kilode? Why are you people shouting?"

My father's face darkened, his jaw tightening as he finally spoke. "Mide is pregnant."

Granny gasped, her frail hands clutching the armrest of the wheelchair. "Olórun má jé!" she muttered, shaking her head. "A pregnant child under my roof? Mide, ó dájú pé iwọ?"

I swallowed hard, tears burning my eyes. "Yes, Granny," I whispered.

Aunty Dunni shifted uncomfortably, trying to find the right words to say. "Sister, please…" she began, but Mum held up her hand, silencing her as wiped the tears of her face.

"So, that's it then," Mum said, shaking her head slowly, her hands open as if trying to grasp something invisible. "All this time, you were meeting with men while pretending to be serious with your studies?"

"Mummy, it's not like that," I tried to explain, but the look on her face told me to stop. She was slowly advancing towards me, her expression hardening.

"Then how is it?" she asked, each word measured, her eyes boring into mine. "Explain to me, Mide. How did this happen?"

I took a step back, my voice failing me. "It's not what you think…"

"It's not what I think? Tell me what I think. Or you didn't sleep with a man? None of your sisters brought this kind of shame to this house, but you… I should have known it would be you to disgrace this family like this."

"Toke." Granny said firmly, gripping my mother's hand. "That is enough. You are her mother, and this is the time she needs you the most, or are we to throw the child away with the bath water?"

Mum exhaled sharply, pulling away. "Mama, do you think I should clap for her? Thank her for this news?"

"Toke, no child should be spoken to like that. Let's all calm down so we can handle this properly,"

My father said finally, placing the newspaper on the coffee table beside him. His voice was calm but firm. I was relieved he had finally spoken, but I couldn't read his emotions. Was he angry or was he disappointed?

"Thank you, my brother," Aunty Dunni added softly.

"Oh, so now you two are teaming up?" Mum turned on her, her voice dripping with sarcasm. "Birds of a feather, abi? You've become her role model, teaching her how to live this life, right?"

Mum knew how to dwell on people's mistakes. It hurt hear her speaking the way she did, especially to dad and Aunt Dunni.

"Toke, please," my father's voice was firm. "Watch your words before you say something you'll regret."

"Regret? What do I have to regret?" she retorted, her voice breaking. "Have I done wrong by Mide as a mother?"

With that, she rushed at me, her hands trembling as she grabbed my arms. "What did I do wrong, Mide? Where did I fail you? What have I done to deserve this?" Her voice was desperate, almost pleading, and I could see tears forming in her eyes again. I was taller but that didn't stop her from grabbing me.

Granny stood, her frail hands reaching out to hold my mum's. "Please, my child, let go of her," she said, her voice carrying authority despite its softness. "You are in pain, but pain does not give you the right to inflict the same on your own."

Mum froze, her fingers loosening before she slowly pulled away, pressing her hands against her face.

I stood there, taking it all in, feeling the weight of her pain in each word she hurled at me. "I'm sorry, Mum," I whispered, tears streaming down my face. "I didn't mean to hurt you."

"Sorry?" she echoed, her voice shaking. "Who is responsible for this?" Her eyes searched my face, but I couldn't bring myself to answer. "Answer me! Who is the father of this child?"

I glanced at my father, who was watching me intently. "Mide, you need to tell us. Who is responsible?" he asked gently.

I shook my head, feeling the tears burn behind my eyes. "I can't say."

"What do you mean you can't say?" Mum's voice rose, filled with disbelief. "Do you not know who you were with?"

I shook my head again, feeling my heart pound in my chest. "I need to speak to him first. I need to know where he stands before I tell anyone else."

My mother's face turned ashen. "Did he force you?" she asked suddenly, her voice trembling with horror. "Were you forced?"

"No!" I shouted, the word tearing out of me. "No, it wasn't like that." My voice was thick with emotion, and I struggled to get the words out. "Please don't ask me who it is. I just need time to figure things out."

"You're protecting him?" Aunty Dunni asked gently, her eyes searching mine.

"No, I'm not." I sobbed. "I just want to speak to him first before I bring everything out in the open."

My grandmother placed a hand on my mother's shoulder. "She is still your child, Toke. She has made a mistake, but she is not lost. Let her find her way."

Mum exhaled shakily. "What are you saying, Mama? If he could be with her, he should be ready to take responsibility."

"That we all calm down and deal with this as a family." Granny said, trying to maintain her cool as well.

I felt my knees go weak, my voice barely a whisper. "Please, just give me some time."

My father walked toward my mum and tried to hold her, but mum kept struggling, wanting to break the hug.

"Toke, mama is right. No child of ours will beg any man. Let Mide speak to him first, and then we will deal with it together."

Mum pulled away from his touch, her shoulders slumping as she buried her face in her hands. "Timi, I don't know how we got here. I just don't know."

"It will be okay, Toke. We will figure it out." my father said gently, his voice calm and reassuring.

Mum stood up abruptly, tears streaming down her face. "I need to go upstairs," she said, her voice was low. I almost didn't hear what she said.

Dad let her go, watching as she left the room, her shoulders shaking with quiet sobs.

"I'll go with her." Aunty Dunni said, giving me a small, supportive smile before following Mum out of the room.

Dad watched them leave before he motioned for me to sit beside him. His face was lined a worry I had never seen. "Mide, I'm not going to pretend I'm happy about this. It's not what your mother and I wanted for you. For any of you, but I won't force you to tell us who the father is, not until you're ready."

I nodded, a wave of gratitude swelling in my chest. "Thank you, Daddy. I'm keeping the baby, no matter what." My voice was steady, though inside I was trembling. Those words weren't just for him — they were a declaration, a warning that I would stand my ground even if it meant standing alone.

He looked at me, and to my surprise, a small smile tugged at his lips. "I'm proud of you for that. It's a brave decision. We will support you through this, however we can."

Granny leaned forward in her chair, her warm voice filling the room. "You won't do it alone, my dear. A child is a blessing, no matter how they come. Your father is right. We may not be happy, but we must choose to see the good in every situation."

Isioma squeezed my hand, her eyes shining. "See? You have all of us. And you have me, always."

Tears blurred my vision as relief washed over me, softening the hard edges of the day. "Thank you, Daddy. Thank you, Granny. Thank you, Isioma," I whispered, my voice breaking on her name.

Dad nodded, his voice firm but gentle. "Go and get some rest, Mide. All will be well."

I climbed the stairs slowly, exhaustion pressing down on me like a heavy cloak. Isioma walked with me; her arm hooked through mine.

I was grateful for Isioma.

She was a steady force beside me.

When we passed my parent's room, I paused. Through the door, I heard the soft, broken sound of my mother's crying. Aunty Dunni sat beside her, murmuring words of comfort, her voice low in the darkness.

My chest ached. I knew it would take time for her to come to terms with this. She and I had never been close, but this — this was the worst wound I could have given her. I hadn't even realized until that moment how deeply I carried my mother's pain, how much I longed for her forgiveness.

Isioma squeezed my arm gently. "Give her time," she whispered. "She loves you more than you know. She'll come around."

Her words wrapped around me like a blanket. And as I finally slipped into my room, Isioma trailing close behind, I knew the battle wasn't over. It had only just begun.

CHAPTER NINETEEN

Life at school wasn't easy.

I would be lying if I said I expected it to be.

Still, I was glad it was almost over as every corridor felt like a battlefield, whispers trailed behind me when I walked into class. Being unmarried and visibly pregnant was enough to feed the gossip mill.

It was tough, but I managed.

On some days, I wished Isioma and Halima were there with me, but the reality was always in front of me. Isioma was back in Nsukka and Halima had left us.

One night, I cried hard, clutching my pillow as though it could offer me comfort.

"Halima, I miss you," I whispered between sobs. "You would have known what to do if you were here."

The next day, desperate to shield myself, I purchased an engagement ring. With a steady face, I told anyone who cared to listen that I had gotten married over the holidays.

It quieted the whispers, but not the loneliness.

Kemi, one of my course mates, became an unexpected blessing. We had never been close, but she showed up bringing assignments and updates when I couldn't attend classes. She was the kind of person you kept close. With her quiet kindness, I crawled through the rest of the semester until graduation finally arrived.

The auditorium was already packed when we arrived.

I had worked so hard to get to this point and was proud that I had made it.

My graduation gown felt unbearably heavy and very uncomfortable. My stomach had grown, rounding out beneath the robe, a constant reminder of the life ahead. Scanning the crowd, I found my father's proud smile and Aunty Dunni's enthusiastic wave. Relief washed over me. Aunty Amaka, elegant as ever in her flowing kaftan, was there too, her bright smile warming the room. Mum was also present, but her demeanour was different.

When I received my certificate, she clapped politely — yet her eyes never met mine.

The sting of that distance cut deeper than any whisper at school.

After the ceremony, we gathered outside to take photos. Laughter and congratulations swirled around me and for a moment, I let myself relax and take it all in.

Dad beamed, placing his arm proudly around my shoulder. "You did so well, my girl. I'm proud of you."

I nodded quickly, blinking back tears. "Thank you, Daddy."

Aunty Dunni slipped beside me, whispering, "Smile, darling. You deserve to shine today." She squeezed my shoulder reassuringly, reading the sadness I tried to hide.

Aunty Amaka handed me a gift bag. "Congratulations, my dear. You've made us all proud. This is from Tife and the gang."

Memories of Tife's easy laughter and Aunty Amaka's fussing over him flashed in my mind, filling me with a strange mix of envy and admiration. "Thank you, Aunty," I murmured, my voice thick.

As more pictures were taken, I noticed Isioma standing at the edge of the group, waving at me excitedly. She had managed to slip in quietly, her wide grin lighting up her face. When she reached me, she hugged me tight. "Mide, I'm so proud of you. I knew you'd make it."

Her words steadied me, like they always did. "Thank you," I whispered, clinging to her.

But the ache returned when my eyes found Mum again. She stood a little apart, chatting with another parent, smiling easily at them though she barely looked my way.

"Mum?" I approached quietly, keeping my voice low. "I just wanted to say thank you for coming. It means a lot to me."

She turned, her face unreadable. "Of course, why wouldn't I come. Congratulations Mide, you've made us proud."

The smile she gave me was small, polite, but her eyes slid away almost instantly as she returned to her conversation.

The lump in my throat grew, as I walked back to Isioma, swallowing hard, until Aunty Dunni caught my eye and pulled me into a warm hug. "Your mum will come around. Don't let it break you. You're amazing, Mide. Remember that."

Isioma came to stand beside us, nodding firmly. "She's right. You've done what many wouldn't even dare to do. Don't let anything steal your joy."

I clung to their words, trying to focus on the joy of the day but deep down, the ache of my mother's silence lingered, coupled with my longing for Demola, it was enough to kill my mood.

* * *

They say when it rains, it pours.

In my own case it was pouring heavily.

At my next appointment I discovered I was having twins! Twins! Demola doesn't know I am pregnant, for some reason, Aunty Amaka, Tife and Labisi didn't tell him.

Labisi was blunt and told me that it would kill Demola to know I had been intimate with another man, so she was going to spare her brother the heartbreak.

If only she knew.

I hadn't even told him I was pregnant and now, I discover I am having twins.

I stared at the screen, completely stunned.

Two tiny figures were visible, their heartbeats flickering like miniature stars. A surge of emotions swirled within me and my hand instinctively moved to my belly, as if to confirm the reality of what I was seeing.

"Twins," I whispered, more to myself than to the doctor. "I'm going to have two babies."

"That's right," he said gently. "You're a bit further along than we originally thought, but everything is progressing beautifully. You should be prepared for some additional challenges that come with a twin pregnancy, but from what I see here, you and the babies are doing just fine."

My mind raced.

I had been worried about having one baby, and now there were two to think about. "Doctor, I still don't want to know the genders," I said, my voice trembling slightly.

He raised an eyebrow but nodded. "That's perfectly fine. We'll respect your decision. Just keep taking good care of yourself, and we'll monitor everything closely to make sure all goes smoothly."

I nodded, still dazed, as he handed me the printout of the ultrasound. Two small figures side by side. Two tiny shadows of life.

For a moment, I couldn't breathe. My eyes traced the blurred outlines again, as if staring long enough would make it real. Two heartbeats. Two futures. Inside me.

Pride swelled in my chest, fierce and startling, but fear quickly followed, sharp and heavy. How could I, who barely felt ready for one, now carry two?

"Thank you, doctor," I murmured, standing slowly. My legs felt weak, as though they might give way under the weight of the news. "I need to sit down."

He gave me a kind, smile. "It's a lot to take in, I know. But you're going to be a wonderful mother, Mide. Don't doubt that."

I nodded, gripping the printout so tightly the edges crumpled in my hand. My heart was racing as I stepped out of the room, the image burning in my mind — proof that my life had just changed again, in ways I hadn't even begun to imagine.

* * *

I entered Aunty Dunni's living room, clutching the ultrasound printout. She was on the sofa, flipping through a magazine, sunlight streaming through the curtains, giving the room a warm glow.

"Aunty," I called softly, my voice trembling.

She looked up instantly, sensing something was different. "Mide, what's wrong? Is everything okay?"

I hesitated, then handed her the printout. "Aunty, I went for my check-up today… I'm having twins."

Her eyes widened as she took the paper, a mixture of surprise and joy lighting her face. She stood and hugged me tightly. "Twins? Oh, my darling! That's wonderful news!"

I exhaled a breath I hadn't realized I was holding. "I'm still trying to wrap my head around it."

"Double the blessing, double the love, double the joy," she said, her excitement infectious. "Don't worry, my dear. We'll figure it out together. You've got all of us."

Her words brought me a deep sense of relief. "Thank you, Aunty. I really needed that."

* * *

That evening when I got home, I decided to tell my parents about my visit to the doctors. Walking to the living room, I offered up a silent prayer hoping that Mum wouldn't pass out from my news. Dad sat in his favourite armchair, reading the newspaper while Mum was on the sofa, flicking through tv channels for a program for she and Granny to binge watch..

"Granny, Daddy, Mummy, I have something to tell you," I began, my voice trembling slightly. Mum turned down the TV volume, a small sign that she was listening.

Dad folded his newspaper and looked at me expectantly. "What is it, Mide?"

I took a deep breath. "I went to the doctor today… and I found out that I'm having twins."

Dad's eyes widened. "Twins? Two babies?"

"Yes, Daddy," I said, a small smile breaking through my nerves. "Two babies."

"That's… wonderful news!" he exclaimed, standing and placing a hand on my shoulder. "Double the joy, double the blessings. I'm so happy for you, Mide."

Granny leaned forward, her eyes bright with emotion. "Olórun ooo! Twins! The Lord has doubled your portion, my dear."

I felt tears well up. Having their support meant everything, especially when Mum still refused to fully acknowledge me.

I glanced at Mum. Her eyes flicked briefly to my belly but stayed mostly on the TV. "Mum… I'm having twins."

Her reply was clipped. "Good for you. I hope this gets better for you."

I swallowed the sting and nodded. "I'll do my best, Mummy. I promise."

Dad cleared his throat, trying to lighten the mood. "Well, we should probably start thinking of names, right? Two little ones to name now."

We began suggesting names, joking about baby supplies and where the twins would sleep. Gradually, Mum's shoulders relaxed slightly. She still avoided direct eye contact, but her quick glances and her faint smiles gave me hope.

I laughed, the sound feeling strange but comforting. "Not really, Daddy. I'm just trying to get through this period."

"We'll figure it out. Don't worry," he said, eyes twinkling.

The room felt warmer, lighter. The tension that had hung so heavily over us all began to ease. I finally allowed myself to believe that things could get better, that Mum would come around eventually.

After the initial excitement at my news had passed, Granny wheeled herself closer to me and rested her hands gently on mine.

"Omo mi," she said softly, her voice steady but warm, "Two little blessings… that's double the love, double the joy. We will face everything together."

I nodded, feeling the weight of her words. "Thank you, Granny. I really needed to hear that."

She gave me a small, knowing smile. "Your father is proud. And your mother… she'll come around. Mothers have a way of showing love quietly, even when it seems hidden and you know that your mother has always been very stubborn."

I glanced at Mum who was still avoiding my gaze, but I noticed something new, a slight softness in her posture, a fleeting glance toward me and Granny as if she were listening more closely than before.

Granny leaned back, wheeling herself toward Mum gently. "My dear, I know this is a lot to take in. But your child… she's going to be a wonderful mother. And these little ones? They're going to need both of you."

For a moment, the room was quiet. Then she let out a slow breath and finally said, her voice quieter than before, "I… I just hope I can do right by them."

Granny reached out and patted her hand softly. "You will Toke; We will. Together."

I felt a small flicker of hope. It wasn't everything, but it was enough to hold onto.

For the first time that evening, the room felt like it could be a home for all of us — a place where support, love, and even quiet acceptance could coexist.

* * *

The day Demola came back was the day I went into labour.

I am sure it was the shock of facing him, heavily pregnant that caused me to go into labour. I was standing in the kitchen when I heard Aunt Dunni chatting on the phone and then she said "Ah, Demola is back, he is bringing you to see Mide, ah that's good, Labisi, she will be happy to see you."

I wasn't ready to face him.

My heart raced, my mind spun, and then suddenly, a sharp, unrelenting pain tore through my lower abdomen. I gasped, then I screamed, clutching my stomach, as my knees buckled underneath me.

"Aunty… it's happening!" I cried, my voice shaking.

Aunty Dunni reacted instantly, racing out of the kitchen to wear I stood, trembling and drenched in sweat.

"Aunty…." I began but then I felt another sharp pain and screamed holding on to the staircase, as my contractions ripped through me again.

"Ah! Cecilia!" my aunt shouted calling for her PA who was working in her study "Hold on, Mide! We are going to the hospital. You're going to be fine." Aunty Dunni said as she gripped my arms. "Àh, Mide, ó má ṣòro.! We're going to the hospital. You're going to be fine."

She guided me to my feet, supporting my weight as I wobbled with each contraction, tears streaming down my face. Cecilia, her PA, appeared just then, quickly moving to help steady me from the other side.

Together, they guided me step by step down the hallway, their hands firm but gentle, making sure I didn't collapse.

Once we got to the driveway, they eased me into the car, with Aunty Dunni supporting my back and Cecilia holding my arm, both kept me upright as I gripped the door handle, trying to suppress the panic rising in me. Each step, each motion, sent waves of pain through me, but their steady presence anchored me enough to get into the car safely.

The drive was a blur of contractions, sweat, and stifled cries as I pressed my face into the seat, trembling with every wave of pain.

My hands clawed at Aunty Dunni's, gripping her like a lifeline.

"I want my mummy!" I screamed, the words ripping from my throat. "I need her! I can't do this without her!"

"She's on her way, darling. Just breathe," Aunty Dunni said, keeping her voice calm and firm. She rubbed my back, whispered prayers, and tried to anchor me through the storm of pain.

But each contraction left me convulsing, gasping, wishing desperately that my Mum was here.

Tears streamed down my face. "Please… Mummy! Where is she? I can't… I can't do this alone!" I felt so helpless, so raw, as if my body were betraying me.

"She's coming," Aunty Dunni repeated, her voice unwavering. "You're strong, Mide. You've got this. Just a little longer."

By the time we reached the hospital, I was nearly hysterical. Nurses rushed me onto a stretcher, and the antiseptic smell of the delivery room burned through my senses.

Every contraction was worse than the last, leaving me trembling and soaked in sweat.

"Breathe, Mide! Breathe In… out… in… out, like you were taught." Aunty Dunni chanted, guiding me as I swayed and screamed. But still, all I could think about was Mum.

"I want my mummy! Mummy, please! I can't do this without her!" I cried, clutching at the air, my nails digging into Aunty Dunni's hands.

At last, as though God had heard my cries of pain, the door swung open and my Mum appeared, her eyes wide, her face tight with worry as she raced to my side.

Relief and fear collided in me, and I reached out for her as another contraction hit, causing me to scream.

"I'm here, my darling," she said, wrapping her hands around mine. Her touch was gentle, almost reverent, and for a fleeting moment, I felt a thread of calm. "Breathe Mide. You are doing so well."

Aunty Dunni whispered fervent prayers beside me, her voice steady, carrying me through the pain. "Lord, protect her. Let these babies come safely into the world. Give her strength. Lord, Fun un ni agbara, Oluwa."

My body shook as the doctor guided me through each push, one wave, one breath, one scream at a time. I cried out in agony as I convulsed, but Mum's hands were there, holding me, whispering encouragement.

Then the first cry came, sharp, tiny, and urgent.

My daughter had arrived, perfect and alive and angry we had disturbed her little world, before I could catch my breath, the second contraction surged again, ripping through me with such force, I thought I would explode.

Another push, another scream, and then my son's cry filled the room. He was smaller, but perfect. Leaning back, I lay against my pillows and burst into tears.

Mum stayed beside me, holding my hands as I was cleaned up and then when they placed my daughter in my arms, she was there to guide me, as I fed my daughter for the first time "They're beautiful," she whispered, leaning close. "So beautiful."

I mouthed silently, "I'm sorry, Mummy. For everything."

"I'm sorry too," she whispered back as pressed a kiss to my forehead that was slick with sweat.

Relief, forgiveness, and love washed over me.

It wasn't perfect, but it was real. Mum, who had seemed so distant for months, was here. She was holding me, supporting me, witnessing the most vulnerable and miraculous moment of my life. For the first time in a long while, as our eyes met, I felt our bond begin to mend. I looked at my babies, their tiny faces scrunched up, and realised that despite every fear, every struggle, I had made it. My babies were here, safe and alive, and my family — Mum, Dad, and Granny — were with me, holding me up when I had needed them the most.

* * *

"Mide"

I looked up from breastfeeding one of the twins and saw my mother standing beside Aunty Dunni, her face etched with emotions she rarely showed. I have always known my mother to be strong, stoic, and at times, critical of me but today, there was something else.

Something tender.

"Thank you, Dunni," I heard her say quietly, her voice full of sincerity. "Thank you for being here for her when I couldn't."

It was such a simple sentence, but it carried so much weight. A lump formed in my throat. Had she ever thanked Aunty Dunni like this before? I wasn't sure. But to hear it now, in this moment, meant everything. The resentment and bitterness that had clouded our relationship seemed to lift, just a little.

Aunty Dunni smiled warmly, squeezing my mother's hand. "We are family, sis. We all do what we can. And look at these two little miracles. Mide did so well."

"She did," Mum agreed, glancing at me and then at the babies. "I was so angry, so afraid for her. But she's stronger than I gave her credit for."

Her words brought tears to my eyes.

I looked down at my son, still feeding, his tiny hand gripping my finger as if to anchor himself. My heart swelled. They were my strength now, these two little lives that depended on me for everything.

"I've been so foolish, Dunni," Mum continued, her voice breaking. "I almost let my pride and anger destroy my relationship with my daughter. But I'm glad you were there, even when I wasn't."

"It's never too late, sister mi," Aunty Dunni said gently. "What matters is that you are here now. You can still be the mother she needs."

Mum nodded and for the first time in what felt like forever, she looked at me with eyes that weren't filled with disappointment or judgment, but with a warmth that made me want to cry all over again.

"I'm sorry, Mide," she said softly, stepping closer. "I'm sorry for everything I said—and didn't say—for not being there when you needed me most."

I held my son tighter. Words failed me, so I just nodded, swallowing the tears threatening to spill.

"I love you, Mum," I whispered, my voice breaking. "I've missed you so much."

"I love you too, my child," she said, her voice thick with emotion. "And I'm here now. I promise—I'll be here for you and for my grandchildren."

We cried quietly then, without the usual tension that accompanied our arguments. It was a different kind of release, a letting go of old hurts, a tentative step toward healing.

Aunty Dunni, always the peacemaker, wrapped us both in a warm hug. "You'll be fine," she said firmly. "These babies are a new beginning. A blessing. Let's focus on that."

We stood together, holding on, united by these tiny lives and the hope they brought. It felt miraculous.

Looking at my mother, my aunt, and my two beautiful babies, I felt a surge of gratitude. Life wasn't perfect, it wasn't easy and there was still a lot of work to do.

But for the first time in a long time, I felt truly hopeful.

I glanced down at my son, now drifting off to sleep, and gently placed him beside his sister. Their little faces were serene, perfect. At that moment, turning back to Mum and Aunty Dunni, I felt like I truly belonged. Like I was home.

* * *

Later that afternoon, there was another knock on the hospital door. I looked up to see Aunty Amaka, Labisi, and Demola standing in the corridor, waiting to be let in.

Aunty Amaka's face lit up as soon as she saw me.

"Mide! And look at these little miracles!" she exclaimed, hurrying into embrace me gently, careful around the babies. Her eyes softened as they fell on the twins. "Ah, small Mide has become a mother and just look at how adorable they are!"

Labisi followed closely, grinning from ear to ear as she crouched beside the bassinet, cooing and pointing at the babies. "Oh, my goodness, Mide, they're gorgeous! You've done so well! Ah, labour was painful right?"

Their joy was palpable, wrapping around me like a warm blanket, and for a moment, I almost forgot the tension I had been carrying since I learnt Demola had returned home. I looked at him from beneath my lashes as he had remained by the door, his expression neutral, arms crossed over his chest.

He didn't smile, didn't lean in, like his mother and sister did, just watched me, silent and unreadable.

"Demola" I greeted him

"Mide, it's been a while, I see congratulations are in order."

I felt my chest tighten at his cold response. Seeing him here, so composed, so controlled, stirred a whirlwind of feelings I hadn't fully confronted: fear, guilt, longing. I had run out on him avoiding him after that night and because of my actions, everything between us had changed.

To make matters worse, I hadn't told him about my pregnancy.

I knew we had to speak so I was glad when Aunt Amaka and Labisi left to get some fruits. Demola stepped closer, as soon as they left the room.

"Mide," he said, his voice calm "I need to ask you something."

My heart thumped so hard I thought he might hear it. "Yes?" I whispered, careful not to move too much.

"The babies... are they mine?"

His words hit me like a blow to the chest. I swallowed hard, tears threatening to spill as I realised, I couldn't lie to him. I had been dreading this moment, imagining every possible reaction he might have—anger, betrayal, heartbreak.

I wasn't sure how he would react, I could only hope he would understand my reasons for keeping my pregnancy from him, but then did I really have a reason?

I forced myself to meet his gaze. "Yes," I said softly. "They are yours."

He studied me, the silence stretching between us, and my guilt rose heavier with each passing second. "You… you ran out on me last time without giving us a chance to talk things over," he said finally, his tone low, controlled. "I find out you were pregnant from Labisi, and I knew immediately that I got you pregnant. What I don't understand, is why you didn't tell me."

I bit my lip, the sting of shame making my chest ache as he spoke, he was right, I hadn't been fair to him, and I know deep down I had hurt him; I could see that now as he looked at me with eyes full of hurt.

Jesus! What have I done?

"I was scared," I admitted, my voice trembling. "I wasn't sure of your reaction, and I was afraid, afraid of losing you, afraid of ruining everything before it even began. You did nothing to make me avoid you Demola, I ran because I was scared."

His eyes softened slightly, just enough to make my stomach twist.

I hated that my heart still ached at the sight of him, even after all the fear and guilt, I still hoped that we could work things out and be together because that was what I really wanted.

I loved Demola, it had taken me a while to accept that.

I dreaded what he might think of me now and hoped he would be willing to give us a chance,

"I should have known," he said after a long pause. "You shouldn't have kept this from me."

"I'm sorry," I whispered, my voice barely audible, tears spilling over as I glanced down at the twins. "I'm so sorry, Demola… for everything. For keeping them from you, for leaving, for—"

He held up a hand, not quite stopping me, but quieting the flood of words.

His gaze shifted to the babies, then back to me and the pain I saw in his eyes broke me. "You were scared," he said clearly pained. "I get that. But you should have trusted me Mide, I have never given you reason not to."

My son stirred in his cot, his tiny hands curling around my finger, grounding me.

I looked up at Demola, my heart heavy with longing, guilt, and hope all at once. I wanted him to understand that my running away had never been about not loving him it had been about fear.

Was it too late for us? I wanted to ask but I was scared he would reject me, reject the love I felt for him and reject our babies.

"You cut me out," he said, his voice low but edged with anger. "After we... after we were together, you just ran, you avoided me. You weren't going to give us a chance because I was just an experiment for you! And then you got pregnant, you didn't even have the decency to call me. Mide, I had a right to know!"

My stomach dropped.

I had imagined this confrontation a thousand times, but hearing it now made my heart pound in panic and shame. "I—I was scared," I stammered, "I didn't know how you would react to the news; you were going to be a father."

He shook his head sharply. "Does anyone else know?" His voice was full of hurt and accusation. "Your family... Aunty Amaka, Labisi... do they know these babies are mine?"

"No," I said quickly, a lump forming in my throat. "No one knows. Only me, I didn't tell anyone."

Demola's expression hardened. He ran a hand through his hair, his jaw tight. "You wouldn't because to you I was just a fling. Mide you are selfish and childish. Do you even understand what you've done?"

I opened my mouth, to speak, to explain that it had never been about keeping him away, but the words caught in my throat.

His eyes, usually warm and easy to read, now cut through me like ice.

"You should have trusted me," he said, voice low. "You should have trusted me enough to tell me the truth. Not run away like a child."

Before I could respond, he turned sharply, grabbing his jacket from the chair. "I can't do this right now," he said, his voice full of pain, he sounded like he was holding back tears. "I need... I need to think."

And just like that, he walked out of my room, shutting the hospital door behind him.

I sank back into the chair, clasping my hands in my lap, my chest heavy with guilt and regret as I replayed his words in my head. Demola was right, I was selfish, childish or how else could I explain my actions?

My hands shook, as the tears fell freely now, soaking the front of my white t-shirt.

Seeing him had made me realise How much I missed him, how much I had wanted him to be here, how much I wanted him to know his babies.

Oh God! I wanted to make things right but now; I needed to make things right but how was I going to do that?

Have I ruined the one chance I had at something beautiful?

God help me, I wouldn't know till I spoke to Demola again, I had too, even if it meant I would kneel under the rain in front of their house, I would kneel, till he gave me the chance to make amends.

Chapter Twenty

I sat in my room crying silently after Demola left and that was how Aunty Amaka and My Mum found me when they walked in moments later.

"Mide!" My mum dropped the basket of fruits she was holding and rushed to my side. "What is it?" she asked worried as Aunty Amaka came to sit beside me.

"Demola just left, he left upset with me!" I sobbed.

"Ehen, we saw him leaving the hospital, he looked angry, didn't he?" My Mum said to Aunty Amaka who nodded.

"Yes, he barely acknowledged us as he walked past us, why is he angry? Did you guys have a fight?" Aunty Amaka wanted to know.

I nodded, sniffing my nose as I looked from Aunty Amaka to Mum, my eyes swollen and red from crying. "He is angry with me; I don't think he will ever speak to me again." I wailed, wringing my hands in despair.

"Come on Mide, stop being dramatic, Demola is not like that, he is probably angry you got pregnant out of wedlock as he has always had high hopes for you and again, he was upset when he found out you were pregnant, he didn't even know you were in a relationship."

I nodded, sniffing as I took the tissue, Aunty Amaka was holding and blew my nose noisily into it. Hmm, if only they knew! Well, there was no need hiding the truth from them any longer, Demola knew, and it was only a matter of time before they all found out he was the father of the twins.

Looking down at my hands, I took a deep breath and said quietly, "Aunty Amaka, Mum, Demola is the father of the Twins." There I had said it, let the screaming and shouting begin. I waited, for my Mum to scream but she said nothing, even Aunty Amaka said nothing.

Bewildered, I looked up expecting to see my mum scowling at me, but I was shocked, Mum and Aunty Amaka had a big smile on their faces, then they did the most amazing thing, The two women got up and began dancing as Aunty Amaka started singing a local song about blessings.

My mouth dropped open in shock.

My life was spiralling out of control, and they were here dancing as though they had just won the lottery?

Really?

Clearing my throat, I said quietly; "Mum, Aunty Amaka, are you okay?"

My Mum rushed to me and planted a kiss on her head, her eyes brimming with tears as she hugged me, then continued dancing with Amaka who was really getting down to it. I couldn't believe my eyes, did these women not understand that Demola had walked out of here angry?

What was there to be happy about.

I finally found my voice. "Mum, Aunty Amaka... Demola is angry. He walked out. Didn't you see him walk out of the hospital in anger?"

They both paused just long enough to exchange a look, then burst out laughing. Mum shook her head, still moving to the rhythm. "Don't worry, my dear. Demola loves you."

Aunty Amaka chimed in, dancing as if her song had taken full possession of her. "Yes, my darling. This is what we've been waiting for. You'll see."

I stared at them, my mouth half open. Waiting for this? For Demola to storm out? For him to be furious? The words tangled in my throat. My chest felt tight, as though I'd stepped into someone else's dream and didn't know the script.

What on earth were they talking about?

"Mum, you don't understand. I hurt Demola and I don't think he would ever forgive me!"

My voice cracked on the last word as my eyes filled with tears again, "He walked out without waiting for me to explain."

My Mum stopped dancing and turned to face me, "We didn't know you and Demola had a thing, you will have to explain how you kept that a secret from your aunt and I but we are happy because we are glad its Demola who is the father of the twins than a random stranger, so let us rejoice."

"You surprise me Mum, are you really not angry?"

"Angry ke? Nibo? When we get home, we will deal with your concerns for now, please calm down you just had a baby, no, you just had twins." My Mum scolded me coming to sit on the bed and take my hands in hers. "Mide, I have no fear that you will work this out, you have proven how strong and resilient you are times without number."

Aunty Amaka nodded firmly, placing her hand on my shoulders "Exactly. This is nothing. Don't let fear blind you, let's get you home and rested first before we deal with the issue of you and Demola."

Their certainty only deepened my confusion.

How could they be so sure, when all I could see was the memory of Demola's face twisted in hurt?

The night at the hospital felt surreal.

It was a blur of exhaustion and joy, but the most comforting presence throughout was my mum. She stayed by my side; her usually stern demeanour seemed to have faded with the sight of her grandchildren and the news that Demola was the father of the twins. Even when I drifted off to sleep, I could feel her presence beside me, hear her whispering soft words of encouragement, as if reassuring me that everything would be fine.

When Daddy arrived the next morning to take us home, the mood in the hospital room shifted to one of celebration. He looked radiant, pride etched into every line of his face as he gently took the babies into his strong arms. His smile was broad, and for a moment, he looked like a man who had conquered the world.

Holding the twins, he glanced up at the sky and muttered a few words in gratitude.

"Timi, you finally have a son," Mum said, her voice filled with happiness. There was a sparkle in her eyes, and she stood close to him, one hand resting gently on his arm.

My dad chuckled, and his eyes twinkled as he looked down at the tiny faces peeking out from the swaddles. "Yes, I finally have a son," he said, his voice warm and full of emotion. "But my girls are worth fifty sons, you know."

Mum's face softened, and she squeezed his arm affectionately. "I know. E se oko mi. Thank you, my husband." Her voice was quiet. She seemed smaller, more vulnerable in that moment, her usual fierce demeanour was replaced by a tender gratitude that I hadn't seen in years.

I watched them together, feeling a strange, bittersweet ache in my chest.

It was the first time I'd seen them so united, so genuinely happy. There was a peacefulness in the way they stood there, side by side, gazing at the twins as if they were the answer to every prayer they had ever whispered.

My son was the first male in my father's line, so that meant a whole lot to them.

As I looked at them, holding onto each other while Dad held the babies, I couldn't help but imagine myself in the same position someday with Demola. Would we ever have moments like this? Would he look at our children with the same pride, the same unrestrained love? The thought brought a wistful smile to my face, but it was quickly replaced by uncertainty.

Mum's voice pulled me back from my thoughts. "Mide, are you alright?" she asked, her eyes searching my face. There was a gentleness in her eyes that made me want to cry again.

"Yes, Mum, I'm fine. Just… thinking." I forced a smile, hoping to reassure her.

She nodded, still watching me carefully. "You've been through a lot, my dear. But you are strong, and you will be fine."

"Thank you, Mummy," I whispered, feeling the weight of her words settle over me like a warm blanket. I was grateful for this new balance between us, this unexpected closeness that had sprung up in the wake of the twins' arrival.

"Timi, let's get these little ones home. They need to rest, and so does their mother." My mum said, a smile on her face.

Daddy nodded, still smiling down at the twins. "Rest? They've been doing that for months." His comment made us laugh. "But you are right, let's go home. I can't wait to show them off to the whole world."

We made our way slowly out of the hospital.

Trust Nigerians, other patients and their families turned to look, smiling at the sight of the tiny babies cradled so protectively in their grandfather's arms.

I trailed behind, feeling proud. Some greeted us while others prayed for us. We thanked them as we continued walking out of the hospital.

At the car, Daddy carefully placed the twins in the baby seats that Aunty Dunni had insisted on getting for us. He buckled them in with a level of concentration and care that made me smile.

"You two behave for your grandfather, okay?" he said softly, adjusting the straps. Then he turned to me with the gentlest expression.

"Mide, your Mum and Amaka have told me about Demola." he said. "I know things have been difficult, but you've shown strength beyond your years. A strength I never even expected from you. These children are a blessing, our blessing. Don't ever forget that, As for Demola, give him time, he will come around."

I nodded. My throat was tight with emotion. I blinked rapidly trying to block the tears behind my eyes. "Thank you, Daddy."

He patted my shoulder. "Now, let's get you home."

The ride back home was quiet, I sat in the back seat, lost in my thoughts. Mum kept glancing back at the twins.

She had a small smile playing on her lips that made my heart ache with joy.

When we reached my parents' house, Alaba who was visiting from school was already waiting by the front door as the car drove in. Buzzing with excitement, she ran to the car, chattering and peeking in at the twins, her face alight with joy.

"Mide, you didn't tell us it was twins!" Alaba exclaimed, her eyes wide with surprise. "Imagine my surprise when daddy told us.

My heart felt fuller than it had in a long time as I watched my sister with my babies. I had my family, and I had my children.

Somehow, I would find a way to make it all work.

* * *

That evening, I watched my Mum take charge of bathing the babies. She set a low stool on the bathroom floor, placed her legs over the bathtub, and then carefully cleaned them one by one. I had no idea what to expect, but I watched in awe as she expertly navigated the delicate task, making sure to avoid getting water on their umbilical stumps. The whole process seemed magical. Despite all the movement, both babies stayed asleep.

It was as though; she had some secret motherly trick to keep them calm.

"Why aren't you bathing them properly, Mum?" I asked, my curiosity getting the better of me.

"I am, we just need to be careful around their belly buttons until they heal. This is just to keep them fresh and clean. Don't worry, soon you'll be doing this yourself." she explained, smiling at me over her shoulder.

I laughed nervously. The thought of handling those tiny, fragile bodies made me nervous, but watching her, I felt a bit more confident. After finishing with the babies, Mum turned to me.

"Now, it's your turn," she said, her voice firm but gentle. "Get into that warm water. It will help relax you and ease some of the pain."

I nodded, sinking into the bath she'd prepared for me. The warmth seeped into my sore muscles, soothing the lingering aches from childbirth. It was exactly what I needed. Once I'd finished my bath and eaten dinner, I made my way to the living room where Mum had laid out the table for dinner.

My eyes filled with tears as I realised how supporting my parents were, I knew they had to be disappointed, but they didn't show it, instead, they were rooting for me, supporting me and providing me with all the love I need.

I turned to my mum who was dishing rice into a plate.

"Mum?" I said, it was more of a question, she looked up and smiled.

"Yes?" she said.

"Thank you, Mum, for everything." I whispered, my eyes holding hers.

She looked down at the plate she was holding, then placing it on the table, she came round to envelope me in a hug.

CHAPTER TWENTY-ONE

The next evening, I was seated with Aunty Dunni in the kitchen, nibbling on a plate of freshly sliced fruits while she was chatting animatedly about a new recipe she wanted to try out, though I was nodding along, my mind was elsewhere.

Then the house phone rang, shattering the quiet.

I jumped up immediately. My first thought was that it was Mum, she had gone to her shop to receive a shipment of new clothes and said she would call me to check up on me, so I excused myself and hurried to pick up the phone, while aunty Dunni went to the living room.

"Hello," I said, my voice steady.

"Mide?" The familiar voice on the other end made my heart stop.

It was Demola.

"Hello?" he repeated, and I realized I hadn't responded.

"Hi…hi, Demola," I finally managed to say, my voice trembling.

"That's nice. You recognize my voice, you remember me, interesting." he said. There was a hint of amusement in his tone.

"Please Demola, don't be like this, can we talk," I pleaded trying to sound calm, but my heart was racing and my thoughts a jumbled mess.

"I didn't call you to fight Mide. I called to check on you, Mum said you came back home last night." he paused then, "How are you?"

"I'm good. You?" I stammered, trying to keep my voice steady.

"Great, is it okay to come around?" he said casually, as if this was the most normal conversation in the world.

"Today?" I asked, evidently surprised.

"Yes, now." His words sent a fresh wave of panic through me.

Oh God! Was he coming to tell me that we couldn't be together? Was that why he sounded so nonchalant? He had never spoken to me in this tone before. I closed my eyes, holding back the tears that threatened to fall.

"Mide…hello…are you there?" His voice brought me back to the moment.

"I…I am. Sorry." I struggled to pull myself together.

"Did you hear anything I said?" He sounded concerned.

"Yeah, yeah, I did, yes you can visit now." I said my words tumbling over each other.

"Cool, see you soon." He sounded hesitant, almost unsure, which was a surprise, considering how nonchalant he had sounded a few seconds ago.

"Soon. Yes, soon is good," I said quickly, desperate to end the conversation before I gave anything away.

There was a pause on the line, and I could almost hear his thoughts. "You sound busy," he finally said, his voice gentle, probing.

"Err… not really," I lied. I was a mess, and he probably sensed it.

"You're alright, yes?" His voice was softer now, tinged with concern.

"Yup. I'm great," I lied again, my voice strained.

"Fantastic. I will head over to yours now."

"Okay." I could barely manage the words. My mind was in complete disarray. Demola was coming, after his reaction yesterday, I wasn't prepared to face him, to show him how desperate I wanted to make up with him.

"Mide?"

"I will wait for you in the kitchen; we can talk if that's okay." I mumbled.

"Talk, yes, that's exactly why I am coming to see you." He said before he hung up the phone

* * *

Demola arrived thirty minutes later.

Aunty Dunni Let him into the house, then after we had exchanged greetings, she excused herself and went to the living room to watch TV, leaving Demola and I in the kitchen.

"Are you okay?" he asked as soon as Aunty left, sliding the kitchen door close behind her.

"Yes." I managed to say.

"Would you like to sit down?"

"No, I need a drink, my throat is a bit dry," I said, rubbing my neck. "I'll get some from the pantry."

As I turned to go to the pantry, Demola blocked my way.

I tried to move his hand, but he was stronger than I was. Trapping me wasn't a good idea, that was exactly how I felt—trapped.

And so, my mouth went on a rampage.

"Look, I apologise for not telling you I was pregnant. At least you know now. The truth is you don't have to be here. I will manage just fine. You can get on with your plans—I mean, your life. We won't bother you. I know I'm not what you want—"

Demola pulled me close and silenced me with a kiss.

It was so sudden, yet gentle as he held my face between his hands. After what felt like a lifetime, he broke the kiss and pressed a soft kiss to my forehead.

"I shouldn't have walked out on you the way I did, I was hurt but that's no excuse."

He lifted my chin, so our eyes met.

"Don't you think it's time we talk Mide?"

"Is it because of the children? I mean you can always see them. You don't have to like me or pretend you want to be with me." I started rambling again until he kissed me again.

It shut me up again.

He lifted his head and smiled at me.

"You don't get it, do you Mide?" he murmured.

"Get what?" I whispered, trying not cry.

His smile was soft, almost nostalgic. "You were never just a childhood friend to me, Mide. Not even close. I've always seen you. Always. Even when you felt I wasn't looking, I was. Mide, you have always been in my line of vision."

I swallowed, feeling the weight of his words settle deep in my chest. "But... we never even talked like that. It was games mostly. You never—"

"I never said anything." he finished for me, his thumb grazing my palm. "I know, but Mide how could I? You took off, you never gave me the chance to tell you how I felt. Why did you do that?"

I looked away, remembering the nights I had spent staring at my phone, contemplating sending him a message, wanting to tell him everything, but holding back.

"I was scared," I admitted, my voice barely audible. "Scared of how you'd react, of how everyone would react. Scared of being judged. It was just... easier to avoid you and pretend that nothing happened between us."

Demola let out a short and almost bitter laugh. "You think I wouldn't have been there for you?"

I shrugged. "I didn't know. And I couldn't take that risk."

His grip on my hand loosened slightly. "I should be angry, you know." he said smiling gently after a moment. "For keeping the children from me. For shutting me out. But I can't be. Because I see you, and I get it. I understand why you did it, even if it hurt like hell when you walked out on me."

"Yesterday, you left before I could say anything." I countered in a low whisper.

"I was just hurt, Mide."

I blinked rapidly, trying to stop the tears stinging at the back of my eyes from falling.

"You never had to do this alone, Mide." he continued, his voice gentle but firm. "You don't have to."

A tear slipped down my cheek before I could stop it.

Demola caught it with his thumb, brushing it away with an aching tenderness that made my chest tighten.

"And for the record." he said, tilting my chin up so I had no choice but to look at him, "I don't love you because of the children. I love you because you're you.

Because you're strong, because you're stubborn, because you drive me crazy in the best and worst ways, Mide." He let out a small chuckle. "Because even when you're pushing me away, I can't stop wanting to pull you closer."

I swallowed hard, my heart hammering against my ribs.

"This doesn't feel real." I whispered.

"Shush...can I speak now?" he asked lazily. I nodded because words weren't forming anymore.

"I love you Mide. It is not about the children. I don't know when or how it happened, but I think I have always loved you, it's always been you."

I watched him through eyes as wide as saucers. How could he love me?

I continued staring into his eyes. "How?"

"What?"

"How can you love me?"

"How can you not know Mide?" he asked as he stroked my cheek. "Do you remember when you lost your doll?"

"Doll?" I asked because I was confused. How did we get to the toys department? "Which of them? I had a lot you know."

"The one with that pink house. What's her name again?" he asked rhetorically, tapping his forehead gently with his index finger.

"Oh, Barbie." I answered with a low laugh.

"Yea, that's the one. You never let her out of your sight after that."

"I know. Once was enough. Mummy had to seize her because barbie and I started going to school together." We laughed together. "How come you remember that event?"

Demola chuckled, his hand gently squeezing mine. "How could I forget? You cried your heart out, until I found it and that was when you captured my heart."

I laughed shyly. I was six years old or so and didn't have the details, but Demola seemed to remember it all.

He wasn't done speaking though.

"There are so many times as a teenager, I wish I could just marry you. Of course, it wouldn't have happened then. However, I knew then that there was something between us. When you came to my room on the morning of Kenny's wedding, for some reason, I wanted to kiss you silly." his voice trailed and he laughed gently instead. "I love you Mide."

I touched his cheek lightly as tears filled my eyes.

"Demola, I love you too and I am so sorry for not trusting you enough to tell you how I felt. I see now that I was childish and selfish…." I began but he silenced me by placing a finger against my lips.

"Enough of the apologies, you have a lifetime to make up for it. Now can I meet my babies?" he said, turning to look out of the window to see my father driving into the compound. "Oh shit! Your folks are back!"

"Are you scared?" I teased as he closed his eyes "My parents don't bite."

"I know that babe, now can we go and meet my babies?"

Babe, he called me babe, I felt my heart fill with joy as I realised what that meant, he had accepted me and acknowledged me as his.

"Mide…? Can we go now?" he repeated glancing down at me.

I grinned up at him, my eyes shining; "I thought you would never ask."

***

Demola and I made our way back to the living room, his fingers wrapped securely around mine.

I could feel my heart beat rapidly, as I heard Aunty Dunni, greet may parents. This was it, the moment when we would have to face our parents as a couple and tell them we wanted to be together.

I was scared because I wasn't sure how my parents would react to Demola.

Yes, they were happy for me, but nobody had asked if we had been dating when I took in, they had simply accepted the fact that he was responsible for my pregnancy and moved on.

The moment we stepped in the living room, every pair of eyes landed on us—my parents, and Aunty Dunni who had joined them. The twins were curled up beside their grandparents, their soft giggles filling the air, completely unaware of the tension in the room.

As my met my father's knowing gaze, my legs almost gave way under me.

Why did he look so serious?

Demola let go of my hand and took a small step forward.

"Good afternoon, Uncle Timi, Aunty Toke" He exhaled slowly, as if steadying himself. "I know that words alone can't change the past, but I need you all to know that really I am sorry for all I put Mide through."

Aunty Dunni gave a small nod of approval and winked at me as my parents smiled and acknowledged Demola's greetings.

My father smiled asking Demola to take a sit which he did and continued speaking, "I should have been here. I should have known. I should have done right by Mide from the very beginning." He hesitated, then glanced at me briefly before looking back at my parents. "I want to make it right now. I want to do right by Mide and be the man she deserves"

I barely had time to process his words before he got up from where he was sitting and lowered himself to the ground.

My breath caught in my throat as he went on his knees before my parents.

I didn't even think—I just found myself kneeling beside him. My heart was racing so fast I thought it might give out. The room was silent except for the giggles of the babies.

Daddy sighed, rubbing his temple before speaking. "Demola, you know I have always regarded you as my son, but you must be sure of what you want, this isn't just about saying the right words. Do you understand the weight of what you are asking for?"

Demola didn't hesitate.

He looked at me, causing my heart to swell in my chest. "Yes, sir. I am sure, which is why I don't want to waste time in making Mide a responsible woman and being the best husband and father to our babies."

Then, he turned to face my father completely, looking him directly in the eye.

"Uncle Timi, you have said it. I am already your son. So please, grant me this wish to marry your daughter."

The words slammed into me causing my mouth to drop open in shock.

Okay, I wasn't expecting this so soon after our reconciliation.

My chest tightened, my head spun, and I could hear my own blood rushing in my ears. Oh God! This was a dream come through! Demola wanted to marry me, could life be any better? I turned to look at my father who was quiet, too quiet.

He looked at Demola for a while, then he sighed and said slowly; "Stand up Demola."

Demola obeyed instantly and got to his feet, leaving me kneeling, unable to move. I was shocked beyond words at Demola's marriage request and could not move, even when my dad asked me to get up.

It wasn't until Demola reached for my hand and gently pulled me up with him that my legs moved.

They felt unsteady.

Weak.

Like I had been standing on uncertainty for too long.

Daddy's gaze softened just a little. "Demola, If this is what my daughter wants, then you have my blessing."

"It is! How can you doubt that?" Granny said from the doorway, a big grin on her face as she was wheeled into the living room. "Demola *Omo mi*, about time you and Mide get married."

Mummy burst into laughter as Granny reached over and tapped my dad on the shoulder. "Do you have to ask? This glasses you have on, what are they for?" she snapped, shaking her head at my father who mumbled something about meddling old women.

Aunty Dunni and my Mum began dancing and clapping their hands as my Granny beamed at me, but I was too shocked to say anything. The only thing I could truly focus on was the way Demola was still holding my hand.

He leaned in close. "Come with me," he murmured.

I blinked at him, my mind still reeling. "Where?"

"Just trust me." He said pulling me out of the living room back to kitchen, where closed the door and pinned me against the wall.

"Demola…" I began.

But he shook his head and said softly, "I've been dying to kiss you properly since yesterday, Babe."

Babe, he called me babe again, I really liked the sound of that.

"So, what are you waiting for? Kiss me please!"

And kiss me he did.

Chapter Twenty-Two

Six Months Later

Today was my wedding day.

I still couldn't believe it.

I was marrying Demola Adetokunbo.

Demola, who had watched me grow from a little girl into a woman, into a mother in my twenties. Demola, who had been my anchor, my strength when I was raped, when I felt I had nothing to live for.

Demola, who had taught me what it meant to love and be loved.

I was marrying Demola, the love of my life.

We would have gotten married the month he proposed, as we didn't want to wait but Aunty Amaka had insisted we wait until after Tife's engagement. "Two weddings in two months would be too much for me to handle," she told us.

So, we waited and it was torture, pure torture, because Demola had insisted on no intimacy till our wedding night.

"I'm waiting for our wedding night, Mide, be patient,"

And so, I waited, and I cursed him every day, but he didn't give in. Irritated, I poured all my energy into helping him decorate his new house in Nicon Town. Demola was back in Nigeria as his company had transferred him home for three years before his next posting, probably to Norway or Aberdeen.

Wherever it was, we would go together, as an expat family.

An expat family.

Me—Mide, an expat wife, hmm, I am still waiting to wake up from this dream.

As my sisters, Lola, Alaba, Kenny, and Taiye, fussed over me in my Vera Wang gown, my eyes filled with tears.

I had come such a long way.

Two months ago, I finally told my sisters about my rape. I would never forget the way Lola and Taiye wept brokenly, as we all held each and cried. After that, the bond between us deepened and for the first time, I felt free.

Two hours later, as I walked down the aisle, I smiled as I saw Demola waiting for me. If anyone had told me years ago that this day would come, I would have shut them up. Turning to glance around the packed church, I caught sight of Isioma in her burgundy bridesmaid dress, and fresh tears stung my eyes.

Isioma my bestie, she was here, but Halima wasn't.

Sweet, beautiful Halima.

I missed her deeply, we both did.

"*Don't forget me.*" She had said.

And I wouldn't, I would never, which was why I had insisted our daughter Temi's second name be Halima. No one had argued, as they all knew how much I needed that.

Halima's parents had been so emotional when they arrived for my wedding two days ago and introduced to my daughter, Temi Halima Adetokunbo.

Lifting my eyes to the ceiling, I whispered a short prayer for Halima, who had urged me to follow my heart and to tell Demola how I truly felt.

I had taken her advice, and he was mine.

*   *   *

The music from the organ, swelled as I reached Demola.

His eyes remained locked on mine, as my father handed me over to him.

My heart rammed into my chest as his hand reached for mine.

I watched mesmerised as he raised my hands to press a kiss against my knuckles, and my fingers trembled as we turned to face the priest who began the ceremony of joining us together as man and wife.

When it was time to recite my vows, my voice shook as I pledged to love him and be loyal to him. Loyalty, a life of laughter, and peace and I honestly meant every word. By the time he spoke his vows, I was crying openly, at his beautiful words that made my heart melt.

"You're my heart, Mide," he said lovingly, not caring that everyone could hear. "You're my beginning and my forever and I will love you forever."

A murmur ran through the congregation, but I barely noticed, I was so caught up in the moment that I almost missed the priest's pronouncing us man and wife and asking him to kiss the bride.

Yes, this was the moment I had been waiting for, the kiss that would proclaim to everyone that I belonged to him. As his lips touched mine, gentle but sure, the church erupted into applause, laughter, and joy.

But for me, it perfect.

His arms around me as he kissed me deeply, and I knew without a doubt that every pain, every loss, every broken piece of me had led to this moment of wholeness and I was grateful for it.

We did it.

We finally did it, we got married!

Demola broke this kiss, his eyes shining with tears as he looked down at me.

"Mide, Tonight, we begin the rest of our lives." He whispered.

And I knew he was right.

* * *

I was nervous.

I stood in the bathroom in our hotel room, clad in the bathrobe provided.

This was our wedding night, and I had just had a bath.

Demola had run me a bath and got me to soak in it after he had a shower. He said and I agree that I looked tired and a soak in there would do wonders for my body. Now I was standing here nervous while my husband ordered dinner for us, I hadn't been able to eat at the reception, between feeding the twins and greeting guests, I just hadn't had the chance to eat.

"Mide, dinner is here." Demola said breaking into my rambled thoughts.

"I'm coming." I said taking a deep breath I turned to leave the bathroom; God knows I wasn't in the mood to eat; I had been waiting for this night for the past six months.

I just had to muster the courage to go for what I want.

Demola was standing by the bed clad only in his pyjama bottoms when I emerged from the bathroom and the sight of him caused my mouth to go dry. Suddenly memories of the night we made love, came back with a vengeance.

Did he think I was going to eat?

No, I wasn't hungry for food, I knew what I wanted, and it was not food.

He turned just I walked up to him, his eyes widening when he saw that I had untied my bathrobe.

"Hey." He said nodding towards the food on the table. "Are you hungry?" I nodded.

"Good, I ordered a lot as I wasn't sure what you wanted." he said just as I slid the bathrobe off, leaving me naked before him. I smiled in satisfaction as his eyes darkened with desire.

"I am hungry Demola but not for food." And before he could say anything else, I reached up, pulled his head down, capturing his lips in an open-mouthed kiss.

It took Demola a split second to react to my kiss.

His arms closed round me as he lifted me off my feet and carried to the bed. Placing me down on the bed, he slid of his trousers before he joined me on the bed, kissing me hungrily.

I kissed him back wrapping my legs around him as he began kissing his way down to my breasts, which were still sensitive as I was breastfeeding, taking a nipple in his mouth, he began sucking on it, as his fingers slid down between my thighs and deep into me.

"Oh God!" I screamed, throwing my head back as he began to work his fingers deep within me all the while sucking and kissing my breasts. My hands moved all over his toned body, kneading, and squeezing and when my hand touched his abdomen, he held my hands, lifting his head from my breasts, he said quietly, "Tonight is about you Mide."

Then he bent his head and continued sucking my breasts as his hands continued to work me, by the time his head replaced his hands I was wet as he used his tongue to do wicked things to me.

I came with force, trembling as I felt myself explode.

Demola, didn't stop, he continued to kiss and suck, even when I came, and when I couldn't bear it any longer, I pulled him up to kiss him tasting myself on his tongue.

"Mide, damn, you taste so good," he said as he nibbled my lips.

Then suddenly, he moved onto his back, lifting me up to straddle him.

Then holding my waist, he slid into me pulling me down slowly to take in all of him.

I threw my head back as I began to move.

I could feel the pleasure building again as he sat up and squeezing my breast, took a nipple in his mouth, sucking as I moved, taking him deeper into me, just when I was about explode, he flipped me on my back and began to thrust into me.

I gripped him hard, moving with him, matching his thrusts as he kissed me, deeply.

"You're my wife now," he whispered against my mouth, which was swollen from his kisses. "You are mine, Mide and I belong to you."

Tears stung my eyes. "Yes," I moaned with pleasure as he kissed me deeply again. "I'm yours Demola."

He groaned, at my words, burying his face in my neck, he began to move fast, thrusting hard, making me weak with pleasure, that was building up deep within me, and then I shuddered as I climaxed, shouting his name as he groaned and followed shortly, emptying his seed deep into me.

* * *

The first light of morning sun spilled through the curtains, painting the room in gold.

I stirred awake, smiling as I saw that my head was resting on Demola's chest. For a moment, I didn't move. I just listened, listened to his breathing.

I listened to the sound of my own heart, calm in a way it had never been before.

I was Demola's wife.

Last night had been fantastic, Demola and I had made love repeatedly. It was as if we were making up for the time, we had been apart.

We couldn't get enough from each other.

I loved the way he had worshipped my body; no part of my body had been spared, I felt warm when I thought of the things he did to me. The thought of how he had kissed me all over, sent a smile creeping across my face.

I felt light, almost weightless, as if the years of pain, of fear, of shame had finally been lifted from me.

Demola stirred slightly, his arm tightening around me.

Even in sleep, he refused to let go of me.

That simple gesture made my throat tighten with tears. For years, I had prayed for safety, for love that did not demand or take but gave and healed. I had prayed for Demola to want me, to love me.

Now here I was with Demola, lying next to me, holding me, loving me.

I traced the lines of his arm with my fingertips, marvelling at the familiarity of him. Last night had not just been about passion, it had been about promise, about love.

Every kiss we had shared had been a language of its own, one only we understood.

It was a language, written in patience and years of waiting.

And now, in the morning light, I felt changed.

I felt loved, my body still tingled from the force of his lovemaking.

I thought of the girl I used to be, broken, and unloved. The girl who thought she would never be enough, never be wanted, never be safe after she had been raped. If I could, I would reach back in time and tell her; "*One day, Mide, you will lie in the arms of a man who adores you, and you will finally know peace.*

Tears slipped down my cheeks, but they were not sad tears.

They were tears of joy.

Demola's voice, rough with sleep, broke into my thoughts. "You're crying, Mide," he murmured, his thumb brushing my cheek.

I turned to look up at him; his eyes were filled with concern.

I shook my head quickly, smiling through the tears. "They're good tears."

He studied me for a moment, then pulled me closer until his forehead rested against mine.

"I love you," he whispered, "And I will spend the rest of my life proving it."

My heart swelled at his words.

"I know," I whispered back. "And I'll spend mine loving you."

He leaned over and kissed me again, his hands pulling me under him as he made love to me slowly, showing me with tender kisses how he felt about me. The love he felt for me was in his touch, in is kisses.

As I nestled against him again, I smiled.

This was it.

This was the beginning of the rest of my life.

I'd finally stepped out of the shadows and for the first time in forever, I was not afraid.

My name is Eyimofe Olamide Idowu Adetokunbo, and this is my story.

ACKNOWLEDGEMENTS

First and foremost, I give thanks to God, whose grace and guidance made this journey possible.

Bringing my debut book to life has been a journey I will always treasure, and I am deeply thankful to those who made it possible.

To my family and friends, your patience, encouragement, and faith in me has been amazing. I could not have done this without your love and support.

So here goes;

To Dafe, my better half, for cheering me on every time I almost gave up. I do not take you for granted.

A special thank you to O.L. Obonna, whose generous review of this book filled me with confidence as a new author. Your words of encouragement reminded me why I began this journey in the first place.

To Sarah Alile, whose support and encouragement meant so much to me along the way.

I am profoundly grateful to the editorial team at Pageleaf Publishing LTD, especially Ayyoub Benebri whose dedication, expertise, and guidance has helped shape this manuscript into its final form.

And finally, to every reader who will choose to spend time with my book, I say a big thank you in advance

www.ingramcontent.com/pod-product-compliance
Lightning Source LLC
Chambersburg PA
CBHW071205070526
44584CB00019B/2921